Editor
Dona Herweck Rice

Editorial Project Manager
Dona Herweck Rice

Editor-in-Chief
Sharon Coan, M.S. Ed.

Illustrator
Sue Fullam

Cover Artist
Barb Lorseyedi

Art Coordinator
Kevin Barnes

Imaging
Alfred Lau
Rosa C. See

Product Manager
Phil Garcia

Publisher
Rachelle Cracchiolo, M.S. Ed.

Comprehension & Critical Thinking

LEVEL 1

Includes Document-Based Questions

Author

Mary Rosenberg

Reading passages provided by *TIME For Kids* magazine.

Teacher Created Materials, Inc.
5301 Oceanus Drive
Huntington Beach, CA 92649
www.tcmpub.com
ISBN-0-7439-3371-0

©2002 Teacher Created Materials, Inc.
Reprinted, 2005
Made in U.S.A.

Table of Contents

Introduction

Comprehension is the primary goal of any reading task. Students who comprehend what they read have more opportunities in life as well as better test performances. Through the use of interesting grade-level nonfiction passages followed by exercises that require vital reading and thinking skills, *Comprehension and Critical Thinking* will help you to develop confident readers who can demonstrate their knowledge on standardized tests. In addition you will promote the comprehension necessary to form the basis for a lifetime of learning.

The articles in *Comprehension and Critical Thinking* present facts about the contemporary world as well as the past. Document-based questions for each passage give your students practice in the newest trend in standardized testing. The students respond to a critical-thinking question based on the information gleaned from a given document. This document is related to the passage it accompanies. Document-based questions show a student's ability to apply prior knowledge and his or her capacity to transfer knowledge to a new situation.

The activities are time-efficient, allowing students to practice these skills every week. To yield the best results, such practice should begin at the start of the school year.

Students will need to use test-taking skills and strategies throughout their lives. The exercises in *Comprehension and Critical Thinking* will guide your students to become better readers *and* test-takers. After practicing the exercises in this book, you will be pleased with your students' comprehension performance, not only on standardized tests, but with *any* expository text they encounter—within the classroom and beyond its walls.

Preparing Students to Read Nonfiction Text

One of the best ways to prepare students to read expository text is to read a short selection aloud to them daily. Reading expository text aloud is critical to developing your students' ability to read it themselves. Since making predictions is another way to make students tap into their prior knowledge, read the beginning of a passage, then stop, and ask them to predict what might occur next. Do this at several points throughout your reading of the text. By doing this, over time you will find that your students' ability to make accurate predictions greatly increases.

Of course, talking about nonfiction concepts is also very important. Remember, however, that discussion can never replace reading aloud because people rarely speak using the vocabulary and complex sentence structures of written language.

Questions help students, especially struggling readers, to focus on what's important in a text. Also, remember the significance of wait time. Research has shown that the amount of time an educator waits for a student to answer after posing a question has a critical effect on learning. So after you ask a student a question, silently count to five (or ten if you have a student who struggles to get his or her thoughts into words) before giving any additional prompts or redirecting the question to another student.

Readability

All of the articles used in this series have been edited for readability. The readability score was obtained from the Flesch-Kincaid grade-level score. This formula determines the grade-level reading skill required to read the text. The formula uses the average sentence length (the number of words divided by the number of sentences) and the average number of syllables per word (the number of syllables divided by the number of words) to determine the reading grade level. (Note: Readability, in the case of nonfiction, is affected by certain unavoidable proper nouns and specialized vocabulary. Please be aware of this when using the articles in this book.)

What Do Students Need to Learn?

Successful reading requires comprehension. Comprehending means having the ability to connect words and thoughts to knowledge already possessed. If you have little or no knowledge of a subject, it is difficult to comprehend an article or text written on that subject. Comprehension requires motivation and interest. Once your students start acquiring knowledge, they will want to fill in the gaps and learn more.

In order to help students be the best readers they can be, a teacher needs to be familiar with what students need to know to comprehend well. A teacher needs to know Bloom's levels of comprehension, know how to formulate document-based questions, know the traditional comprehension skills and expected learning outcomes, and know the methods that can be used to help students build a framework for comprehension.

Bloom's Taxonomy

The questions that follow each passage in *Comprehension and Critical Thinking* assess all levels of learning by following Bloom's Taxonomy, a six-level classification system for comprehension questions devised by Benjamin Bloom in 1956. The questions that follow each passage are always presented in order, progressing from knowledge to evaluation.

The skills listed for each level are essential to keep in mind when teaching comprehension to assure that your students reach the higher levels of thinking. Use this classification to form your own questions whenever your students listen to or read material.

Level 1: Knowledge—Students recall information or find requested information in an article. They show memory of dates, events, places, people, and main ideas.

Level 2: Comprehension—Students understand information. This means that they can find information that is stated in a different way than the question. It also means students can rephrase or restate information in their own words.

Level 3: Application—Students apply their knowledge to a specific situation. They may be asked to do something new with the knowledge.

Level 4: Analysis—Students break things into their component parts and examine those parts. They notice patterns in information.

Level 5: Synthesis—Students do something new with the information. They pull knowledge together to create new ideas. They generalize, predict, plan, and draw conclusions.

Level 6: Evaluation—Students make judgments and assess value. They form an opinion and defend it. They can also understand another person's viewpoint.

Introduction *(cont.)*

Document-based Questions

It is especially important to guide your students in how to understand, interpret, and respond to document-based questions. For these questions, in order to formulate a response the students will have to rely on their prior knowledge and common sense in addition to the information provided in the document. Again, the best way to teach this is to demonstrate through thinking aloud how to figure out an answer. Since these questions are usually interpretive, you can allow for some variation in student responses.

The more your students practice, the more competent and confident they will become. Plan to have the class do every exercise in *Comprehension and Critical Thinking*. If you have some students who cannot read the articles independently, allow them to read with a partner, then work through the comprehension questions alone. Eventually all students must practice reading and answering the questions independently. Move to this stage as soon as possible. For the most effective practice sessions, follow these steps:

1. Have the students read the text silently and answer the questions.

2. Have the students exchange papers to correct each other's multiple-choice section.

3. Collect all the papers to score the short-answer question and the document-based question portion.

4. Return the papers to their owners and discuss how the students determined their answers.

5. Refer to the exact wording in the passage.

6. Point out how students had to use their background knowledge to answer certain questions.

7. Discuss how a child should explain his or her stance in each short-answer question.

8. Discuss the document-based question thoroughly.

Standardized Test Success

One of the key objectives of *Comprehension and Critical Thinking* is to prepare your students to get the best possible scores on the reading portion of standardized tests. A student's ability to do well on traditional standardized tests in comprehension requires these factors:

- a large vocabulary
- test-taking skills
- the ability to cope with stress effectively

Test-taking Skills

Every student in your class needs instruction in test-taking skills. Even fluent readers and logical thinkers will perform better on standardized tests if you provide instruction in the following areas:

Understanding the question: Teach students to break down the question to figure out what is really being asked of them. This book will prepare them for the kinds of questions they will encounter on standardized tests.

Concentrating on just what the text says: Show students how to restrict their response to just what is asked. When you go over the practice passages, ask your students to show where they found the correct response in the text.

Ruling out distracters in multiple choice answers: Teach students to look for the key words in a question and look for those specific words to find the information in the text. They also need to know that they may have to look for synonyms for the key words.

Maintaining concentration: Use classroom time to practice this in advance. Reward students for maintaining concentration. Explain to them the purpose of this practice and the reason why concentration is so essential.

Practice environmental conditions throughout the year in order to acclimate your students to the testing environment. For example, if your students' desks are usually together, have students move them apart whenever you practice so it won't feel strange on the test day.

Some other ideas for "setting the stage" whenever you practice include the following:

- Put a "Testing—Do Not Disturb" sign on the door.
- Require no talking, active listening, and following directions during practice sessions.
- Provide a small strip of construction paper for each student to use as a marker.
- Give each student two sharpened pencils and have a back-up supply handy. Tell the students to raise a broken pencil, and you will immediately provide them with a new one.

Coping with Stress

Teach students to recognize their apprehension and other stressful feelings associated with testing. Give students some suggestions for handling stress, such as taking a deep breath and stretching.

At the beginning of the school year start talking about good habits like getting enough rest, having a good breakfast, and daily exercise. Enlist parental support by sending home a letter encouraging parents to start these good habits right away.

Remember to let students stretch and move around between tests. Provide a physical release by running in place or playing "Simon Says" as a stress-buster during practice sessions throughout the year as well as on the test day.

Build confidence throughout the school year by using the practice passages in this book. Do not include the passage scores in the students' class grades. Instead, encourage your students by having them complete the "Student Achievement Graph" on page 108, showing how many questions they answered correctly for each practice passage. Seeing their scores improve or stay consistently high over time will provide encouragement and motivation.

On the test day, promote a relaxed, positive outlook. Tell your students to visualize doing really well. Remind them that since they have practiced so much, they are thoroughly prepared.

Teaching Nonfiction Comprehension Skills

Nonfiction comprehension encompasses many skills that develop with a lot of practice. The following information offers you a brief overview of how to teach the crucial skills of recognizing text structure, visualizing, summarizing, and learning new vocabulary. This information is designed for your use with other classroom materials, not the practice passages in *Comprehension and Critical Thinking*.

Introduction (cont.)

You will find many of these skills in scope-and-sequence charts and standards for reading comprehension:

- recognizes stated main idea
- identifies details
- determines sequence
- recalls details
- labels parts
- summarizes
- identifies time sequence
- describes character
- retells information in own words
- classifies, sorts into categories
- compares and contrasts
- makes generalizations
- draws conclusions
- recognizes text organization
- predicts outcome and consequences
- experiences an emotional reaction to a text
- recognizes facts
- applies information to a new situation

Typical Comprehension Questions

Teaching the typical kinds of standardized test questions gives students an anticipation framework and helps them learn how to comprehend what they read. It also boosts their test scores. The questions generally found on standardized reading comprehension tests are as follows:

Facts—questions based on exactly what the text states: who, what, when, where, why, and how many

Sequence—questions based on order: what happened first, last, and in between

Conditions—questions asking students to compare, contrast, and find the similarities and differences

Summarizing—questions that require students to restate, paraphrase, choose main ideas, conclude, and select a title

Vocabulary—questions based on word meaning, synonyms and antonyms, proper nouns, words in context, technical words, geographical words, and unusual adjectives

Outcomes—questions that ask readers to draw upon their own experiences or prior knowledge, which means that students must understand cause and effect, consequences, and implications

Opinion—questions that ask the author's intent and require the use of inferencing skills

Document-based—questions that require students to analyze information from a source document to draw a conclusion or form an opinion

Introduction *(cont.)*

Teaching Text Structure

Students lacking in knowledge of text structure are at a distinct disadvantage; yet this skill is sometimes overlooked in instruction. When referring to a piece to locate information to answer a question, understanding structure allows students to locate quickly the right area in which to look. Students also need to understand text structure in order to make predictions and improve overall comprehension.

Some children have been so immersed in print that they have a natural understanding of structure. For instance, they realize that the first sentence of a paragraph often contains the main idea, followed by details about that idea. But many students need direct instruction in text structure. The first step in this process is making certain that students know the way that authors typically present ideas in writing. This knowledge is a major asset for students.

Transitional paragraphs join together two paragraphs to make the writing flow. Most transitional paragraphs do not have a main idea. In all other paragraph types, there is a main idea, even if it is not stated. In the following examples the main idea is italicized. In order of frequency, the four types of expository paragraph structures are as follows:

1. **The main idea is often the first sentence of a paragraph. The rest of the paragraph provides the supporting details.**

   Clara Barton, known as America's first nurse, was a brave and devoted humanitarian. While caring for others, she was shot at, got frostbitten fingers, and burned her hands. She had severe laryngitis twice and almost lost her eyesight. Yet she continued to care for the sick and injured until she died at the age of 91.

2. **The main idea may fall in the center of the paragraph, surrounded on both sides by details.**

   The coral have created a reef where more than 200 kinds of birds and about 1,500 types of fish live. *In fact, Australia's Great Barrier Reef provides a home for many interesting animals.* These include sea turtles, giant clams, crabs, and crown-of-thorns starfish.

3. **The main idea comes at the end of the paragraph as a summary of the details that came before.**

   Each year Antarctica spends six months in darkness, from mid-March to mid-September. The continent is covered year-round by ice, which causes sunlight to reflect off its surface. It never really warms up. In fact, the coldest temperature ever recorded was in Antarctica. *Antarctica has one of the harshest environments in the world.*

4. **The main idea is not stated in the paragraph and must be inferred from the details given. This paragraph structure is the most challenging for primary students.**

   The biggest sea horse ever found was over a foot long. Large sea horses live along the coasts of New Zealand, Australia, and California. Smaller sea horses live off the coast of Florida, in the Caribbean Sea, and in the Gulf of Mexico. The smallest adult sea horse ever found was only half an inch long!

Introduction *(cont.)*

Teaching Visualization Skills

Visualization—seeing the words of a text as mental images in the mind—is a significant factor setting apart proficient readers from low-achieving ones. Studies have shown that the ability to generate vivid images while reading strongly correlates with a person's comprehension of text. However, research has also revealed that *20 percent of all children do not visualize or experience sensory images when reading.* These children are automatically handicapped in their ability to comprehend text, and they are usually the students who avoid and dislike reading because they never connect to text in a personal, meaningful way.

Active visualization can completely engross a reader in text. You have experienced this when you just could not put a book down, and you stayed up all night to finish it. Skillful readers automatically weave their own memories into text as they read to make personalized, lifelike images. In fact, every person develops a unique interpretation of any text. This personalized reading experience explains why most people prefer a book to its movie.

Visualization is not static; unlike photographs, these are "movies in the mind." Mental images must constantly be modified to incorporate new information as it is disclosed by the text. Therefore, your students must learn how to revise their images if they encounter information that requires them to do so.

Sensory imaging—employing any of the other senses besides sight—is closely related to visual imaging. It too has been shown to be crucial to the construction of meaning during reading. This is because the more senses that are employed in a task, the more neural pathways are built, resulting in more avenues to access information. You have experienced sensory imaging when you could almost smell the smoke of the forest fire, taste the sizzling bacon, or laugh along with a character as you read. Sensory imaging connects the reader personally and intimately to the text and breathes life into words.

Since visualization is a challenging skill for one out of every five students to develop, begin with simple *fictional* passages to scaffold their attempts and promote success. After your students have experienced success with visualization and sensory imaging in literature, they are ready to employ these techniques in nonfiction text.

Visualization has a special significance in nonfiction text. The technical presentation of ideas in nonfiction text coupled with new terms and concepts often overwhelm and discourage students.

Using visualization can help them to move beyond these barriers. As an added benefit, people who create mental images display better long-term retention of factual material.

Clearly there are important reasons to teach visualization and sensory-imaging skills to your students. But perhaps the most compelling reason is this: Visualizing demands active involvement, turning passive students into active constructors of meaning.

Doing Think-Alouds

It is essential for you to introduce visualization by doing think-alouds to describe your own visualization of text. To do this, read aloud the first one or two lines of a passage and describe what images come to your mind. Be sure to include *details that were not stated in the text,* such as the house has two stories and green shutters.

Introduction (cont.)

Then read the next two lines and explain how you add to or otherwise modify your image based on the new information provided by the text.

When you are doing a think-aloud for your class, be sure to do the following:

- Explain how your images help you to better understand the passage.
- Describe details, being sure to include some from your own schema.
- Mention the use of your senses—the more the better.
- Describe your revision of the images as you read further and encounter new information.

Teaching Summarizing and Paraphrasing

Summarizing informational text is a crucial skill for students to master. It is also one of the most challenging. Summarizing means pulling out *only* the essential elements of a passage—just the main idea and supporting details. Research has shown that having students put information into their own words causes it to be processed more thoroughly. Thus, paraphrasing increases both understanding and long-term retention of material. Information can be summarized through such diverse activities as speaking, writing, drawing, or creating a project.

The basic steps of summarizing are as follows:

- Look for the paragraph's main idea sentence; if there is none, create one.
- Find the supporting details, being certain to group all related terms or ideas.
- Record information that is repeated or restated only once.
- Put the summary together into an organized format.
- Scaffolding is of critical importance. Your students will need a lot of modeling, guided practice, and small-group or partner practice before attempting to summarize independently. All strategies should be done as a whole group and then with a partner several times before letting the students do it on their own. Encourage the greatest transfer of knowledge by modeling each strategy's use in multiple content areas.

Teaching Vocabulary

In the early years, students may start seeing words in print that they may have never met before in either print or oral language. As a result, these students need direct instruction in vocabulary to make real progress toward becoming readers who can independently access expository text. Teaching the vocabulary that occurs in a text significantly improves comprehension. Since students encounter vocabulary terms in science, social studies, math, and language arts, strategies for decoding and understanding new words must be taught throughout the day.

Students' vocabularies develop following this progression: listening, speaking, reading, and writing. This means that a child understands a word when it is spoken to him long before he uses it in his own speaking. The child will also understand the word when he reads it before he will attempt to use it in his own writing. Each time a child comes across the same word, his or her understanding of that word deepens. Research has shown that vocabulary instruction has the most positive effect on reading comprehension when students encounter the words multiple times. That is why the best vocabulary instruction requires students to use new words in writing and speaking as well as in reading.

Teaching vocabulary can be both effective and fun, especially if you engage the students' multiple modalities (listening, speaking, reading, and writing). In addition, instruction that uses all four modalities is most apt to reach every learner.

Introduction (cont.)

The more experience a child has with language, the stronger his or her vocabulary base. Therefore, the majority of vocabulary activities should be done as whole-group or small-group instruction. In this way children with a limited vocabulary can learn from their peers' knowledge base and will find vocabulary activities less frustrating. Remember, too, that a picture is worth a thousand words. Whenever possible provide a picture of a new vocabulary word.

Selecting Vocabulary Words to Study

Many teachers feel overwhelmed when teaching vocabulary because they realize that it is impossible to thoroughly cover all students' unknown words. Do not attempt to study every unknown word. Instead, choose the words from each selection wisely. Following these guidelines will result in an educationally sound vocabulary list:

- First, choose words that are critical to the article's meaning.

- Then, choose conceptually difficult words.

- Finally, choose words with the greatest utility value—those that you anticipate the children will see more often (*e.g.*, choose *anxious* rather than *appalled*).

These suggestions are given for teaching nonfiction material in general. *Do not select and preteach vocabulary from these practice passages.* You want to simulate real test conditions in which the children would have no prior knowledge of any of the material in any of the passages.

Using Context Clues

Learning vocabulary in context is important for two reasons. First, it makes children become active in determining word meanings, and second, it transfers into their lives by offering them a way to figure out unknown words in their independent reading. If you teach your students how to use context clues, you may eventually be able to omit preteaching any vocabulary that is defined in context (so long as the text is written at your students' independent level).

There are five basic kinds of context clues:

1. **Definition:** The easiest case is when the definition is given elsewhere in the sentence or paragraph.
   example: The ragged, *tattered* dress hung from her shoulders.

2. **Synonym:** Another simple case is when a synonym or synonymous phrase is immediately used.
   example: Although she was fat, her *obesity* never bothered her until she went to middle school.

3. **Contrast:** The meaning may be implied through contrast to a known word or concept. Be alert to these words that signal contrast: although, but, however, even though.
   example: Although Adesha had always been *prompt*, today he was 20 minutes late.

4. **Summary:** Another form is summary, which sums up a list of attributes.
   example: Tundra, desert, grassland, and rain forest are four of the Earth's *biomes*.

5. **Mood:** Sometimes the meaning can be grasped from the mood of the larger context in which it appears. The most difficult situation is when the meaning must be inferred with few other clues.
   example: Her *shrill* voice was actually making my ears hurt.

Police Office Next Door

Ellis Sinclair has 33 kids. He is a police officer. He wanted to help kids with problems.

He moved into a house in the kids' tough neighborhood.

He meets with the kids and the principal of their school. He listens to the kids when they want to talk. It is working. Before, most of the kids had been in trouble. Now only a few are having problems.

Ellis Sinclair thinks his work is more than a job. He wants "his" 33 kids to have a better life. He says, "They are my family." He really lives his job!

Police Office Next Door (cont.)

Directions: Answer these questions. You may look at the story.

1. What kind of job does Ellis Sinclair have?

    a. He is a police officer.

    b. He is a teacher.

    c. He is a fire fighter.

2. Why did Officer Sinclair move into the tough neighborhood?

    a. He wanted to try something new.

    b. He wanted to help kids with problems.

    c. He thought the house was pretty.

3. What kind of behavior did the kids have before Officer Sinclair moved into the neighborhood?

    a. Most of the kids were very shy.

    b. Most of the kids had been in trouble.

    c. Most of the kids played in the street.

4. What do you think will happen to the neighborhood a year from now?

    _____

5. On the back of this page, draw a picture to show what might happen if more police officers moved into the neighborhood.

6. If every student had a police officer living on the same street, what do you think would happen to their behavior?

    _____

7. Is police officers living in tough neighborhoods a good idea? Why or why not?

    _____

8. Explain why you think the kids' behavior improved?

    _____

9. What evidence would show that the kids' behavior improved?

    _____

Police Office Next Door *(cont.)*

Directions: Read the chart. Answer the questions.

	Before Last Year	**After** This Year
Poor Attendance	30 students	4 students
Poor Behavior	29 students	1 student
Poor Grades	27 students	3 students
Not Following School Rules	18 students	6 students

1. What does the chart about the students' behavior show from last year to this year? Why do you think there has been a change?

   _____

   _____

2. Why do you think the attendance has improved?

   _____

   _____

3. What has caused the students' grades to improve?

   _____

   _____

4. What do you think would happen if Officer Ellis moved out of the neighborhood?

   _____

   _____

Working with Mom

I went to work with my mom. She is an accountant. That is a person who works with lots of numbers. Mom's office is on the 53rd floor. Her desk is next to the window. I asked if she was scared she would fall out. She laughed.

"I can see our house from here," I said. My mom didn't believe me.

The phone rang about twelve times every minute. People ran in and out of her office. They carried papers and asked her questions. We went to five meetings. They were not very interesting to me. But my mom seemed to like them a lot.

The office was very noisy. How did she get anything done?

Mom smiled. "Work can sometimes be the hardest place to get work done."

Working with Mom *(cont.)*

Directions: Answer these questions. You may look at the story.

1. Where does the mother work?

    a. She works at home.

    b. She works in a factory.

    c. She works on the 53rd floor.

2. What does an accountant do?

    a. An accountant works with a lot of numbers.

    b. An accountant works with a lot of letters.

    c. An accountant works with a lot of colors.

3. Why do you think the office was noisy?

    a. Barking dogs made the office noisy.

    b. People talking and phones ringing made the office noisy.

    c. Children made the office noisy.

4. Using the information from the story, would you like to be an accountant when you grow up? Explain why or why not.

    _____

5. Explain what the mother meant when she said, "Work can sometimes be the hardest place to get work done."

    _____

    _____

6. Compare and contrast your parent's job to the mother's job? How are the jobs alike? How are the jobs different?

    _____

    _____

7. Why is it sometimes difficult to get work done at school?

    _____

8. Tell why the meetings were interesting to the mother but not to the child.

    _____

    _____

Working with Mom *(cont.)*

Directions: Read the job advertisement. Answer the questions.

We are looking for an accountant. The person needs to do these things:

- know how to use a calculator
- have good math skills
- have an accountant's license
- know how to use a computer
- have 3–5 years experience
- have good "people skills"

This job offers good pay and benefits.

Call us at (123) 555-7890 if you are interested in this job.

---

1. What are some of the skills listed for this job?

   _____

   _____

2. What are good "people skills"?

   _____

   _____

3. What kind of math skills would an accountant need?

   _____

   _____

4. Since the rules and laws regarding money are always changing, what would the accountant need to do to keep his or her knowledge up to date?

   _____

   _____

Directions: Read the story.

The Iditarod's Top Dogs

Doug Swingley raced to the end of the Iditarod Trail Sled Dog Race. Fans were on the streets of Nome, Alaska. It was 1:31 in the morning. It was cold.

Swingley broke two sleds. It did not stop him. He finished 9 hours before the next person.

This is the second time Swingley has won. He won $69,000 and a truck. He and his 11 dogs raced the 1,100 miles from Anchorage to Nome in 9 days.

"I have got to take a long rest," said Swingley. So did his dogs!

The Iditarod's Top Dogs (cont.)

Directions: Answer these questions. You may look at the story.

1. What is the race called?

   a. It is called the Race for Dogs.

   b. It is called the Iditarod Trail Sled Dog Race.

   c. It is called the Nome Alaska Race.

2. What members are on each team?

   a. Each team has 1 person and 11 dogs.

   b. Each team has 11 people and 1 dog.

   c. Each team has 1 person and 1 dog.

3. Describe the Iditarod race.

   a. The Iditarod is an 1,100 mile sled dog race from Anchorage to Nome, Alaska, and it takes about 9 days.

   b. The Iditarod is a 1,000 mile sled dog race from San Diego to Santa Ana, California, and it takes about 9 days.

   c. The Iditarod is an 11,000 mile sled cat race from Anchorage to Nome, Alaska, and it takes about 3 days.

4. Compare the Iditarod race to another kind of race (marathon, Tour de France, car race, etc.). How are the races alike? How are the races different?

   _____

5. What would happen if each team had more dogs or fewer dogs?

   _____

6. Explain why dogs are used to pull the sleds and not horses.

   _____

7. What other animal could be used to travel long distances within a short period of time? What characteristics would make that animal a good choice?

   _____

8. Can any dog be used to pull a sled? Explain why or why not.

   _____

The Iditarod's Top Dogs *(cont.)*

Directions: Look at the map. Answer the questions.

Iditarod for 2003

1. Anchorage
2. Eagle River
3. Chugiak
4. Palmer
5. Wasilla
6. Knik
7. Yentna
8. Skentna
9. Finger Lake
10. Rainy Pass
11. Rohn
12. Nikolai
13. McGrath
14. Takotna
15. Ophir

17. Shageluk
16. Iditarod
18. Anvik
19. Grayling
20. Eagle Island
21. Kaltag
22. Unalakleet
23. Shaktoolik
24. Koyuk
25. Elim
26. Golovin
27. White Mountains
28. Safety
29. Nome

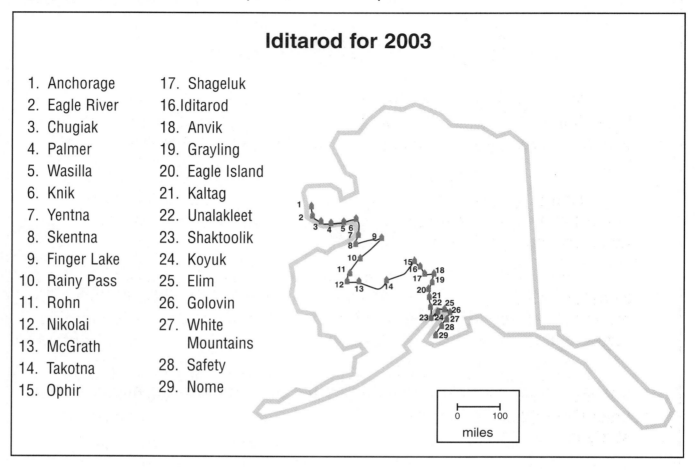

1. Where does the Iditarod begin and end?

   _____

   _____

2. About how far apart are the mile markers? Why do you think the race is divided into shorter sections?

   _____

   _____

3. How does each team find its way from one marker to the next?

   _____

   _____

4. What changes could be made to make the Iditarod an easier race?

   _____

   _____

A Sixth Great Lake

The five Great Lakes are big. They can be seen from space. Lake Superior and Lake Huron are two of the biggest lakes in the world. Lake Ontario is the smallest Great Lake. But it is still very big.

Some people think that Lake Champlain should be the sixth Great Lake. The Great Lakes were made from glaciers. So was Lake Champlain. Rivers link it to the Great Lakes.

Scientists get money to study the Great Lakes. Vermont Senator Patrick Leahy wanted Lake Champlain to get some of that money. In March 1998, a law made Lake Champlain the sixth Great Lake.

Then, some people said Lake Champlain is not a Great Lake. It is too small. So, the law was changed after just 18 days. Now Lake Champlain is not a Great Lake. But scientists will get money to study it.

A Sixth Great Lake (cont.)

Directions: Answer these questions. You may look at the story.

1. Which lakes are two of the biggest lakes in the world?
   a. Lake Superior and Lake Huron
   b. Lake Champlain and Lake Huron
   c. Lake Ontario and Lake Champlain

2. From where can the Great Lakes be seen?
   a. They can be seen from the White House.
   b. They can be seen from space.
   c. They can be seen from glaciers.

3. Describe how the Great Lakes were made.
   a. They were made from space.
   b. They were made from rivers.
   c. They were made from glaciers.

4. How is Lake Champlain like the other Great Lakes?

   _____

   _____

5. Identify the rules for calling a great lake a "Great Lake"?

   _____

   _____

6. What makes the Great Lakes so great?

   _____

   _____

7. Why do you think the senator from Vermont wanted Lake Champlain to be considered a "Great Lake"?

   _____

   _____

8. Should Lake Champlain be a Great Lake? Tell why or why not.

   _____

   _____

A Sixth Great Lake (cont.)

Directions: Look at the map. Answer the questions.

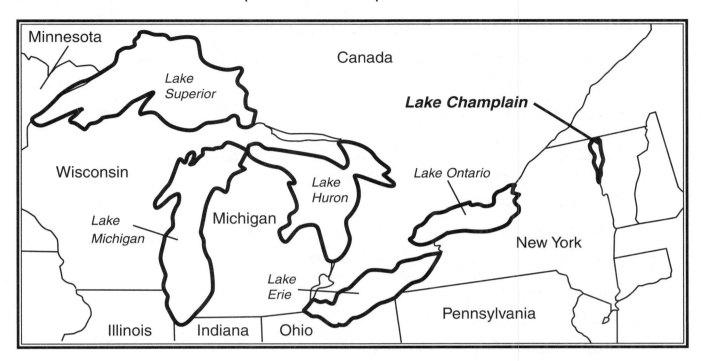

1. What are the names of the five Great Lakes?

   _____

   _____

2. Name the states that surround the Great Lakes.

   _____

   _____

3. Which lake is the smallest? Which lake is the largest? Rank the five Great Lakes in size from smallest to largest.

   _____

   _____

4. What might happen if other states wanted their lakes to be recognized as "Great Lakes," too?

   _____

   _____

The Sound of Old Music

Scientists were digging in China. They found old pots. They found parts of homes. They found 36 flutes.

Each flute had five to seven holes. The flutes were made from bird bones. The flutes were made 9,000 years ago. One of the flutes had no cracks. It could still be played!

The scientists played one of the flutes. The flute is one of the oldest instruments ever played. It is not the oldest flute found. Scientists found a flute made from a vulture bone. It is 33,000 years old.

The Sound of Old Music *(cont.)*

Directions: Answer these questions. You may look at the story.

1. Where were the flutes found?

   a. They were found at the store.

   b. They were found in homes.

   c. They were found in China.

2. What was the oldest flute made from?

   a. It is made from a vulture bone.

   b. It is made from pottery.

   c. It is made from china.

3. Describe how the old flutes were probably made.

   _____

   _____

4. What other instruments played today were first made thousands of years ago?

   _____

   _____

5. Tell how instruments have changed over the years. Tell how instruments have stayed the same.

   _____

   _____

6. How are the old flutes like today's flutes? How are they different?

   _____

   _____

7. Invent a new instrument. What materials would you use? How would it be played? What would it be called? What would it sound like?

   _____

   _____

8. What evidence tells the scientists that the flutes are thousands of years old and not hundreds of years old?

   _____

   _____

The Sound of Old Music *(cont.)*

Directions: Look at the flute. Answer the questions.

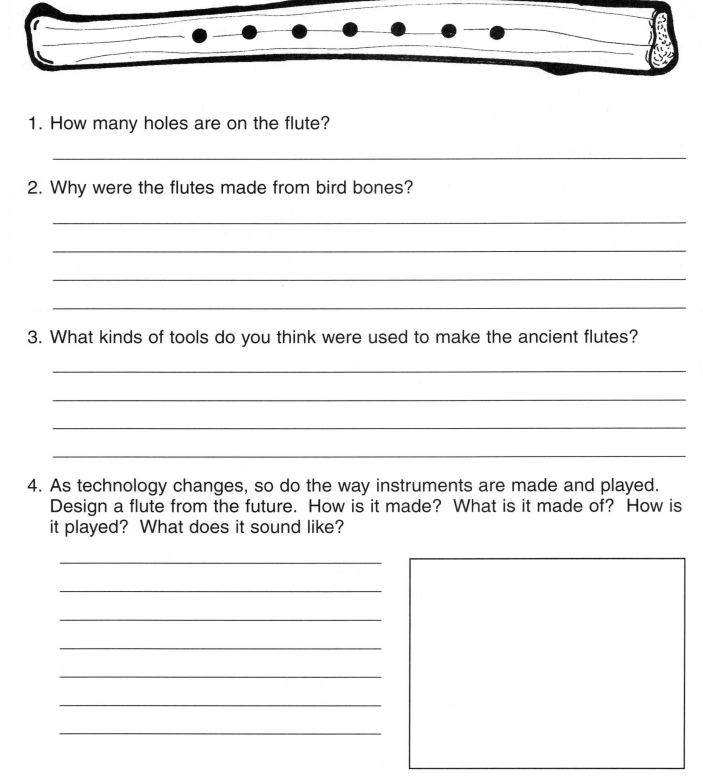

1. How many holes are on the flute?

   _____

2. Why were the flutes made from bird bones?

   _____

   _____

   _____

   _____

3. What kinds of tools do you think were used to make the ancient flutes?

   _____

   _____

   _____

   _____

4. As technology changes, so do the way instruments are made and played. Design a flute from the future. How is it made? What is it made of? How is it played? What does it sound like?

Play With Your Food

Does the stuff that goes into your school lunch make you laugh? These fruits and vegetables will.

The book, *How Are You Peeling?*, by S. Freymann and J. Elffeers, has lots of pictures. They show faces made from food. The faces are made with stems for noses and seeds for eyes. An orange is a laughing head. An onion is a sad face.

The book shows you it is okay to be upset. Look for *How Are You Peeling?* in the library. Use the pictures to make your own faces out of food. For once, Mom may be happy you are playing with your food.

Play With Your Food (cont.)

Directions: Answer these questions. You may look at the story.

1. What is the title of the book?

    a. *Are You Peeling Okay?*

    b. *What Is Your Peeling?*

    c. *How Are You Peeling?*

2. What is the book about?

    a. The book is about feelings.

    b. The book is about oranges.

    c. The book is about being silly.

3. On the back of this paper, draw a picture of yourself when you are happy and sad. What kinds of things make you happy? What kinds of things make you sad? Write a list of items under each face.

4. How do you think the book got its title?

    _____

    _____

5. Why do you think this book was written?

    _____

    _____

6. Why do you think fruits and vegetables were used to make the faces instead of breads, desserts, or meats?

    _____

    _____

7. On the back of this paper, create a new face that shows an emotion. What items were used to create the "head"? What items were used to make the "face"?

    _____

    _____

8. Is this a book you want to read? Explain why or why not.

    _____

    _____

Play With Your Food *(cont.)*

Directions: Look at the picture. Answer the questions.

1. What kind of fruit is shown in the picture?

   _____

   _____

2. What items were used to make the face?

   _____

   _____

3. What emotion is shown on the fruit? How can you tell?

   _____

   _____

4. What are some things that might make the fruit happy?

   _____

   _____

5. How could the items be rearranged or changed in shape to make the fruit look happy?

   _____

   _____

Directions: Read the story.

People Should Not Capture Whales

Have you ever seen a whale at a sea park? It is fun to see the big whales. But people should not keep whales in parks. Whales belong in the sea.

A baby gray whale washed up on a beach in 1997. She was sick and hungry. Workers at Sea World in San Diego helped her. They fed her a drink that was like the milk from a mother whale. The whale's name was J.J. J.J. soon put on weight. She put on about two pounds an hour! Finally, she weighed more than 17,000 pounds. She was 29 feet long. She was healthy.

The Sea World workers did not keep J.J. They put J.J. back into the sea. They knew that other whales would show her how to get food. They knew that whales need to swim all over the sea. Whales should not be kept in water parks.

People Should Not Capture Whales *(cont.)*

Directions: Answer these questions. You may look at the story.

1. What do baby whales eat?

   a. They eat fruit.

   b. They eat fish.

   c. They eat milk from a mother whale.

2. How many pounds did J.J. gain each hour?

   a. She gained about one pound each hour.

   b. She gained about two pounds each hour.

   c. She gained about ten pounds each hour.

3. What did the workers at Sea World do to help the whale?

   a. They fed her and then put her back in the sea in a safe place.

   b. They fed her and kept her at Sea World for everyone to enjoy.

   c. They put her right back in the sea.

4. On the back of this paper, draw a picture of a whale in its natural habitat.

5. Compare the whale's natural habitat to a sea park habitat. How are they alike? How are they different?

   _____

   _____

6. Why did the workers at Sea World release her back into the ocean?

   _____

   _____

7. What do you think would happen if a whale were raised in a sea park and after many years, set free in the ocean?

   _____

   _____

8. Is it right to keep whales in a sea park? Why or why not?

   _____

   _____

People Should Not Capture Whales (cont.)

Directions: Look at the diagram. Answer the questions.

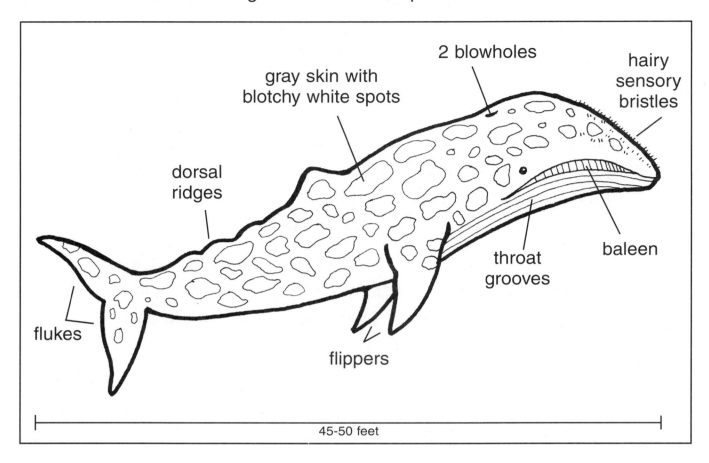

gray skin with
blotchy white spots

2 blowholes

hairy
sensory
bristles

dorsal
ridges

throat
grooves

baleen

flukes

flippers

45-50 feet

1. How long is a gray whale?

_____

_____

2. How can you tell by looking at a whale that it lives in the water?

_____

_____

3. What other animals living in captivity would be better off living in their natural habitats? Why?

_____

_____

4. On the back of this paper, design a sea park for the future. Make each habitat as natural as possible. Do you think this sea park could ever be made? Why or why not?

_____

Gr-r-r-eat News About Tigers

Tigers used to live all over Asia. Hunters had killed many tigers. The tigers' grassy homes were almost gone. The tigers eat deer and boar. The deer and boar were almost gone. People were afraid that the tigers would be gone, too.

But the striped cats are coming back! Two kinds of tigers are coming back. People gave land to the tigers. Now they have land to live on. The tigers have lots of food. The tigers are safe from the hunters. "Tigers are still in danger," says John Seidensticker. "But we have hope. It is a nice surprise."

Gr-r-r-eat News About Tigers *(cont.)*

Directions: Answer these questions. You may look at the story.

1. What are the "striped cats"?

    a. They are lions.

    b. They are pets.

    c. They are tigers.

2. Where did many tigers once live?

    a. They used to live all over the place.

    b. They used to live all over the jungle.

    c. They used to live all over Asia.

3. Explain what has happened to the number of tigers living in the wild.

    a. The number went down because of hunters, and now the tigers are almost gone.

    b. The number went down because of hunters, and now the tigers are coming back.

    c. The number went down because of sickness, and now the tigers are coming back.

4. On the back of this paper, draw a picture of a tiger in its natural habitat 100 years ago. Draw a picture of the tiger's natural habitat today.

5. What caused the population of tigers to decrease? Why do you think this happened?

    _____

    _____

6. Explain why the population of tigers is now beginning to increase.

    _____

    _____

7. What if there were no more tigers left in the world? What would it be like?

    _____

8. Should tigers be saved from extinction?

    _____

Gr-r-r-eat News About Tigers (cont.)

Directions: Look at the graph. Answer the questions.

In the 1900s there were over 100,000 tigers living in the wild. Today there are about 6,000 tigers left living in the wild. The graph below shows approximately how many tigers are left. (The numbers do not include tigers living in zoos.)

Kind of Tiger		Number in the Wild
Balinese	0	
Caspian	0	
Javan	0	
Bengal		4,000
Indo-Chinese		1,400
South China	50	
Siberian	300	
Sumatran	450	

1. Identify the tiger with the largest population. Identify the tiger with the smallest living population (more than 0).

   _____

   _____

2. What has happened to the Balinese, Caspian, and Javan tigers? Why do you think this has happened?

   _____

   _____

3. By the time you are an adult, what do you think will have happened to the population of the South China Tigers? Why?

   _____

   _____

4. What other animals do you know that have become extinct? What events have caused this to happen?

   _____

   _____

Treasures in the Sand

A man was riding his donkey on a road in Egypt. The donkey tripped. The donkey's leg fell into a hole. The man looked into the hole. The man saw many mummies!

The mummies had been there for 2,000 years. A team has dug up 105 mummies.

Charms, pots, and coins were found with the mummies. There may be many more mummies, too!

Treasures in the Sand (cont.)

Directions: Answer these questions. You may look at the story.

1. What did the man find?
    a. The man found donkeys.
    b. The man found mummies.
    c. The man found a hole.

2. How many mummies were found?
    a. 150 mummies
    b. 510 mummies
    c. 105 mummies

3. How long had the mummies been there?
    a. 2,000 years
    b. 200 years
    c. 20 years

4. Who do you think the mummies were?

    _____

    _____

5. What other items do you think might be found with the mummies? Why?

    _____

    _____

6. Why do you think that charms, pots, and coins were buried with the mummies?

    _____

    _____

7. Why were the mummies found in such good shape after so many years?

    _____

    _____

8. Should private collectors be allowed to take things out of the burial sites?

    _____

    _____

Treasures in the Sand *(cont.)*

Directions: Look at the picture. Answer the questions.

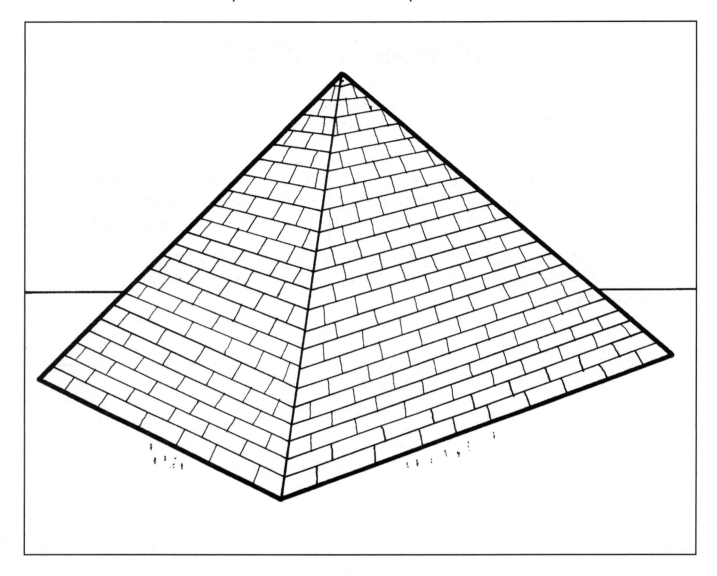

1. What kinds of materials do you think were used to make the pyramids?

   _____

   _____

2. How do you think the heavy stones were moved into place?

   _____

   _____

3. Could pyramids be made today? Why or why not?

   _____

   _____

The Fossil Finder

Sam was 8 years old. He went to see his grandma. His grandma lived in Alabama. They went to a mine. The mine was packed with fossils.

Now Sam is 16 years old. He is a fossil scientist. He helped dig up a *T. rex* skeleton! He also dug up a bone of a mastodon. A mastodon was kind of like an elephant. It was 4$\frac{1}{2}$ million years old!

Sam does not tell other scientists his age. If the other scientists knew Sam was a kid, they would not take his work seriously.

The Fossil Finder *(cont.)*

Directions: Answer these questions. You may look at the story.

1. How old was Sam when he became interested in fossils?

    a. 8

    b. 16

    c. 18

2. Where did Sam find his first fossil?

    a. He found it in his backyard.

    b. He found it in his grandma's backyard.

    c. He found it in a mine near his grandma's house.

3. Compare and contrast a mastodon to an elephant.

    _____

    _____

4. How did finding fossils in the mine change Sam's life?

    _____

    _____

5. Besides dinosaurs, what other things can become fossilized?

    _____

    _____

6. How would scientists know which animal a fossilized bone belonged to?

    _____

    _____

7. What kinds of information can scientists obtain by examining fossils?

    _____

    _____

8. Is it more important to examine fossils to learn about the past or is it more important to develop inventions for the future?

    _____

    _____

The Fossil Finder (cont.)

Directions: Look at the picture. Answer the questions.

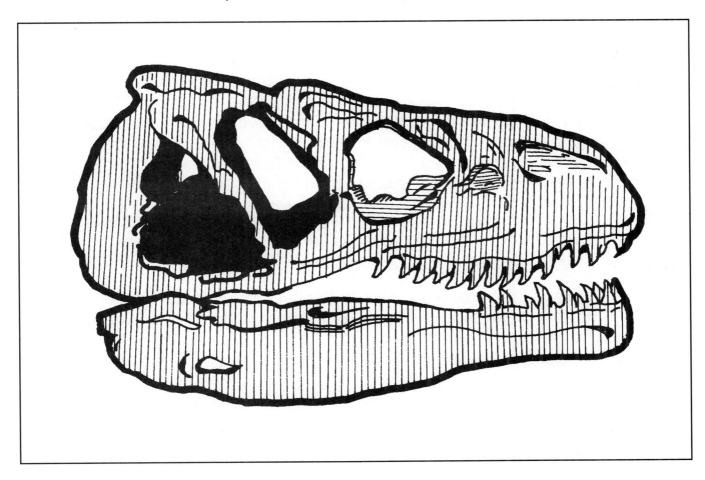

1. What part of the body does the fossil show?

_____

2. Identify the animal the fossil came from.

_____

3. What kinds of information can you tell by examining the fossil?

_____

_____

4. What kinds of animals do you think are still undiscovered and unknown to people? On the back of this paper, draw a picture to illustrate a new kind of animal.

_____

_____

A Lucky Brake

Kids can be real heroes. Larry Champagne, 10, is one. He saved a whole school bus full of kids. The bus driver passed out on the way to school. The bus started to bang into fences along the road. Kids screamed. But Larry ran to the front and stopped the bus. How did he do it? He pushed hard on the brake!

Larry knows about brakes because he helps his grandfather work on his truck. "And my grandmother always tells me to do what's right," says Larry.

Larry's act made news all over the country. He was even on TV. His school gave him a medal. But the kids on that bus already knew he was a real hero.

A Lucky Brake *(cont.)*

Directions: Answer these questions. You may look at the story.

1. How old was Larry when he stopped the bus?

    a. 10

    b. 12

    c. 20

2. Describe how the kids knew there was a problem on the bus.

    a. The bus came to a stop.

    b. The bus driver passed out and the bus banged into fences.

    c. Larry ran to the front of the bus.

3. Compare and contrast buses and trucks.

    _____

    _____

4. How did knowing about trucks help Larry stop the school bus?

    _____

    _____

5. What makes a person a hero? Can anyone be a hero?

    _____

    _____

6. Explain why Larry's actions made the news all over the country.

    _____

    _____

7. What would have happened if Larry hadn't stopped the bus?

    _____

    _____

8. When riding in cars, the passengers have to wear seatbelts. Should students riding on a bus have to wear seatbelts, too? Why or why not?

    _____

    _____

A Lucky Brake (cont.)

Directions: Look at the picture. Answer the questions.

1. Identify the vehicle. Why is it used?

_____

_____

2. What are the different ways students can get off a bus in case of an emergency?

_____

_____

3. Are there any emergency times when it would be safer for students to stay on a bus instead of getting off a bus?

_____

_____

4. What kinds of things could be added to a school bus to make it safer for both the bus driver and the students?

_____

_____

Directions: Read the story.

A New Dinosaur Pair

James Kirkland is a scientist. He went to Utah. He found the bones of two kinds of dinosaurs. The bones had never been seen before.

The bones were in a group called ankylosaurs. They ate plants. They had thick, hard plates. They could grow to more than 30 feet long.

One of the dinosaurs is an ankylosaurid. It had a long tail. There was a club at the end of it. It would swing the tail to fight larger animals.

The other dinosaur is a nodosaurid. It had spikes on its shoulders. "It used to ram bigger animals," says Kirkland.

Scientists thought ankylosaurs came to North America 70 million years ago. But these bones are 25 million years older than that!

A New Dinosaur Pair *(cont.)*

Directions: Answer these questions. You may look at the story.

1. What did James Kirkland discover?

   a. He discovered some animal bones.

   b. He discovered two dinosaurs.

   c. He discovered the bones of two kinds of dinosaurs.

2. When did scientists first think ankylosaurs came to North America?

   a. 7 million years ago

   b. 70 million years ago

   c. 700 million years ago

3. What could the new dinosaurs use to defend themselves?

   a. sharp teeth

   b. long tail with spikes

   c. long tail with a club and spikes

4. Describe an ankylosaur.

   _____

   _____

5. What do you think the enemies of these two dinosaurs might have been like?

   _____

   _____

6. Why do you think these bones are so special to scientists?

   _____

   _____

7. Based on what you know, do you think there are other undiscovered animals out there?

   _____

   _____

8. Explain why it is important to find bones of previously undiscovered and unknown animals.

   _____

   _____

A New Dinosaur Pair (cont.)

Directions: Look at the picture. Answer the questions.

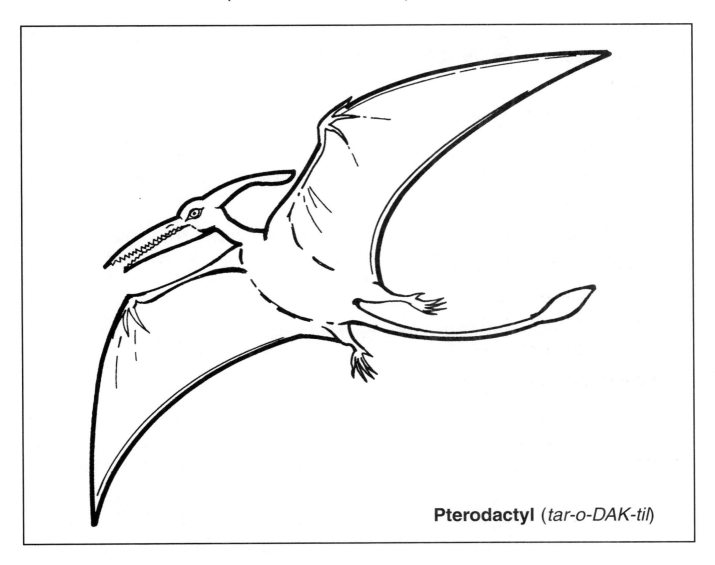

Pterodactyl (*tar-o-DAK-til*)

1. Who do you think were the enemies of this dinosaur?

_____

_____

2. What could this dinosaur do or use to keep itself safe from other dinosaurs?

_____

_____

3. What animal living today is similar to this dinosaur? How are the two animals alike? How are they different?

_____

_____

A Very Cool Hotel

"Welcome to our hotel. Come on in. It is cold!" How would you like to sleep at a hotel made of ice?

There is a hotel in Sweden. It is called the Ice Hotel. The hotel and the beds are made of ice and snow! The temperature of your room is 20°F. Brrr!

Why do people want to sleep on a big ice cube? The hotel manager says, "People like the beauty. It is pure winter. It is white. The snow is fresh. It is very quiet." The 4,000 people who stayed there think so, too.

The Ice Hotel melts into a puddle in the spring. But by the fall, people start making a new one!

A Very Cool Hotel (cont.)

Directions: Answer these questions. You may look at the story.

1. Why is the hotel so cold?

    a. It is under the ground.

    b. It is made of ice.

    c. It has a good air conditioner.

2. What is the "big ice cube"?

    a. It is the hotel.

    b. It is an iceburg.

    c. It is a bed.

3. How does the Ice Hotel compare to a regular hotel? How are they alike? How are they different?

    _____

    _____

4. What other items can be used to make an unusual hotel? On the back of this paper, draw a picture to illustrate the hotel.

    _____

    _____

5. Describe the tools needed to make the Ice Hotel.

    _____

    _____

6. What should you take with you if you were to stay at the Ice Hotel?

    _____

    _____

7. Where could the Ice Hotel be made so it wouldn't need to be rebuilt each year? Would people want to stay there? Why or why not?

    _____

    _____

8. Would you want to stay in the Ice Hotel? Why or why not?

    _____

    _____

A Very Cool Hotel *(cont.)*

Directions: Look at the picture. Answer the questions.

1. What do we call this kind of house?

   _____

2. What materials were probably used to make the house? How was the house made?

   _____

   _____

3. Describe what it is like inside the house.

   _____

   _____

4. Where would this type of house be made? What is the weather like there?

   _____

   _____

5. How long might the house last?

   _____

   _____

Aliens in Lake Victoria

Aliens have taken over Lake Victoria! They are not little green men. They are green plants with purple flowers. The plants are called water hyacinths.

The plant comes from South America. Now it is filling up Africa's biggest lake. No one knows how it got there.

The plants make a huge carpet. The carpet covers the water. The plants trap fishing boats. There are people who live by the lake. The people can not go fishing. The people need the fish for food and money.

Scientists are using little beetles. The beetles eat the plants. Some people used a big machine. The machine is called the *Swamp Devil*. It cuts up the plants. But some scientists are worried. They think it may kill too many of the plants. Some fish in the lake need the plants for food.

Aliens in Lake Victoria *(cont.)*

Directions: Answer these questions. You may look at the story.

1. Where is Lake Victoria located?
    a. South America
    b. Africa
    c. a swamp

2. Who or what needs the plant?
    a. fish
    b. people
    c. aliens

3. Describe a water hyacinth.

    _____

    _____

4. Why do you think the big machine is called the *Swamp Devil?* What other names would be good choices?

    _____

    _____

5. What does the plant do to the lake? How does it impact (or hurt) the people who live by the lake?

    _____

    _____

6. What are the "aliens"? Why do you think they are called that?

    _____

    _____

7. Can you think of any other way to get rid of the plants without hurting the animals that live in the lake and the people who live around the lake?

    _____

    _____

8. Are the water hyacinths good or bad? Explain your reasoning with facts.

    _____

    _____

Aliens in Lake Victoria *(cont.)*

Directions: Look at the picture. Answer the questions.

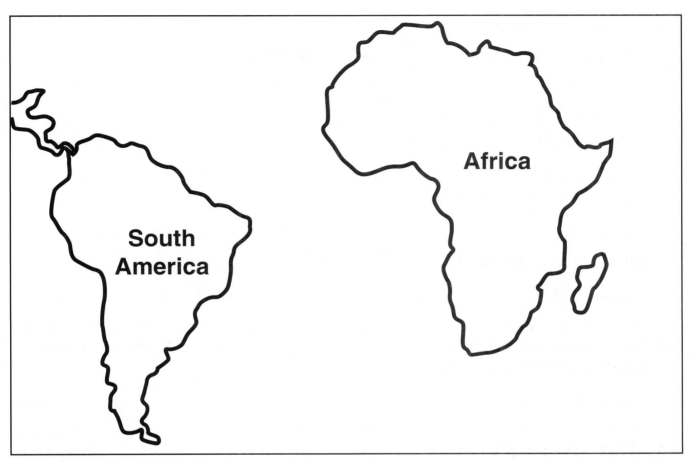

1. What two continents are shown on the map?

   _____

   _____

2. What are the different ways to travel from South America to Africa? Which way would take the most amount of time? Which way would take the least amount of time?

   _____

   _____

3. How do you think the water hyacinth traveled from South America to Africa?

   _____

   _____

4. Predict what might happen if plants from Africa ended up in South America.

   _____

   _____

Squiggle Art

My class went to the art museum. We looked at a painting by a famous artist named Jackson Pollock. It had squiggles of paint running all over it. It made me smile.

"Anyone could make that painting," my friend Susie said. Susie always says stuff like that.

I didn't think it would be that easy. Then I saw a piece of gum stuck to the painting. I reached out to peel it off.

Beep! Beep! An alarm went off. A guard rushed over.

I put up my hands. I shouted, "I'm just trying to clean up the painting!"

The guard smiled. He said, "It's okay. The gum is part of the painting."

Squiggle Art *(cont.)*

Directions: Answer these questions. You may look at the story.

1. Where did the class go?

    a. The class went to the art store.

    b. The class went to the art museum.

    c. The class went to the zoo.

2. Why did the student try to pull the gum off of the painting?

    a. The student wanted the gum.

    b. The student was dared to pull off the gum.

    c. The student wanted to clean up the painting.

3. Compare squiggle art to a picture from a book. How are they alike? How are they different?

    _____

    _____

4. Identify other places that have guards or alarms. What do these places have in common?

    _____

    _____

5. Explain the reasons for having guards and alarms in museums.

    _____

    _____

6. Think of the different kinds of art that you like. Describe the qualities and characteristics that make a picture (or painting, sculpture, craft item, etc.) a "work of art."

    _____

    _____

7. What problems could occur if the visitors were allowed to touch and handle the different items in a museum?

    _____

    _____

8. Do you think squiggle art is really art? Explain your reasoning.

    _____

    _____

Squiggle Art *(cont.)*

Directions: Look at the picture. Answer the questions.

1. What is the artist's name?

   _____

   _____

2. Identify the setting.

   _____

   _____

3. What kinds of materials do you think were used to create the painting?

   _____

   _____

4. Imagine a new painting by Jackson Pollock. What does it look like? What is a good title for the painting?

   _____

   _____

Directions: Read the story.

A Dream Come True

Hannah Kristan did not like recess. "I never got to play. I just sat there," she said.

Now Hannah is 12. She was born with a disease. The disease did not let the bones in her back grow the way most kids' do. She needs a wheelchair. Kids in wheelchairs cannot use the swings and slides.

Hannah heard about special playgrounds for disabled kids. She helped raise money for one in her town. She said, "Disabled kids are just like other kids. We want to play with our friends."

A Dream Come True (cont.)

Directions: Answer these questions. You may look at the story.

1. Why didn't Hannah play on the equipment at recess?
   a. She needs her wheelchair, so she could not use the equipment.
   b. She did not like the equipment.
   c. Mean kids would not let her play on the equipment.

2. Why does Hannah need a wheelchair?
   a. Her feet hurt her.
   b. Her back is too long.
   c. Her back did not grow the way most kids' backs do.

3. What was Hannah's dream?

   _____

   _____

4. What does it mean to be disabled?

   _____

   _____

5. What other kinds of disabilities are there?

   _____

   _____

6. How are disabled children and able children alike? What kinds of things do all children need?

   _____

   _____

7. Make a list of the different kinds of equipment that can be found on most playgrounds. Can each piece of equipment be used by all children? If not, how can that piece be changed so that more children can use it?

   _____

   _____

   _____

8. Why is it important that children with disabilities be able to use the playground equipment?

   _____

   _____

A Dream Come True (cont.)

Directions: Look at the picture. Answer the questions.

1. Where are these people?

_____

_____

2. What are some of the problems the people might have in getting around this place?

_____

_____

3. What changes can be made to make it easy for all people to get around here?

_____

_____

4. What are some other barriers that might prevent a person from playing a game, using a piece of equipment, or just doing everyday things? How can the barriers be removed?

_____

_____

Get Set for Space

What is it like to ride into space? We can tell you about it. We are men and women who will become astronauts.

We have to learn a lot about the spacecraft. We must know how to make everything work. Machines help us, too. They help us work in space.

We might have to fix something outside the spacecraft. We practice in a pool. In space we will float like this, too.

A spacecraft may land in the wrong place. So we learn to take care of ourselves.

We work hard. We do not mind the hard work. Going into space is a dream come true.

Get Set for Space *(cont.)*

Directions: Answer these questions. You may look at the story.

1. Where are the astronauts going?

    a. They are going to school.

    b. They are going to space.

    c. They are going to dinner.

2. How will they get into space?

    a. They will ride a spacecraft.

    b. They will fly a plane.

    c. They will go underwater.

3. Why do the astronauts need to know how to make everything work?

    _____

    _____

4. Why do the astronauts practice fixing things in a swimming pool?

    _____

    _____

5. Make a list of the kinds of things (information) an astronaut would need to know before traveling in space.

    _____

    _____

6. Describe a space suit that contains everything an astronaut needs during a space mission.

    _____

    _____

7. What if one of the astronauts becomes sick or injured? What would the other astronauts do?

    _____

    _____

8. Explain why it is important to explore space.

    _____

    _____

Get Set for Space *(cont.)*

Directions: Read the list. Answer the questions.

Packing List

- 2 shirts with Velcro®
- 2 pairs of shorts with Velcro®
- 4 T-shirts with Velcro®
- 2 pairs of pants with Velcro®
- 1 pair of slipper socks
- 1 flight jumpsuit
- 1 sleeping bag with Velcro®
- food in containers or bags with Velcro®
- food tray with Velcro®

---

1. Name three items an astronaut needs to take into space.

   _____

   _____

2. Why do many of the items have Velcro® on them?

   _____

   _____

3. If you were an astronaut and were going to be orbiting in space for a month, what are some other items you would add to the Packing List? Why would those items be important?

   _____

   _____

4. Many items used today were first made to meet the needs of astronauts. Some of the items are food in squeeze tubes, freeze-dried foods, drinking pouches with a place for a straw, and pre-cooked, individually packed meals. What items do you think will be invented for space trips in the future?

   _____

   _____

It's a Pokémon World

"Got to get them all!" That is what kids said. Kids fell for Pokémon.

The name means "pocket monster" in Japanese. The game is from Japan. The game made a lot of money for the company that made it.

In 1998, the monsters came to America. Kids ate them up. Stores ran out of the games. The TV show was a big hit, too. A company began to make Pokémon cards. It was a good idea. Kids loved trading the cards. 850,000 sets were sold in four months.

It's a Pokémon World *(cont.)*

Directions: Answer these questions. You may look at the story.

1. What does Pokémon mean?

   a. pocket game

   b. pocket men

   c. pocket monster

2. Where did the game come from?

   a. Japan

   b. America

   c. Jordan

3. Do you know how the game is played? Explain it.

   _____

   _____

4. Compare Pokémon to another kind of trading card. How are they alike?
   How are they different?

   _____

   _____

5. Invent a new Pokémon character. Draw a picture of the character on the
   back of this paper.

6. Explain why kids like Pokémon so much. What makes the kids want to
   collect all of the characters?

   _____

   _____

7. Invent a new trading card game and characters. What is the game's name?
   What do the characters look like? What age of kids would like to play the
   game?

   _____

   _____

8. Do you think that ten years from now kids will still be crazy about Pokémon?
   Explain why or why not.

   _____

   _____

It's a Pokémon World (cont.)

Directions: Look at the time-line chart. Answer the questions.

20th Century Toys and Games

1900	baseball cards	**1945**	Silly Putty
1901	ping-pong	**1957**	Frisbee
1902	Teddy bear	**1958**	Barbie doll
1909	jigsaw puzzle	**1960**	Troll doll
1918	Raggedy Ann doll	**1975**	skateboard
1926	miniature golf	**1983**	Cabbage Patch Kids doll
1929	yo-yo	**1989**	Teenage Mutant Ninja Turtle figures
1934	Monopoly	**1990**	rollerblades
1943	Scrabble	**1998**	Pokémon game

1. What year was Monopoly invented?

   _____

   _____

2. Circle the toys that you still play with today. Explain why people still play the same games or use the same toys that were invented many years ago.

   _____

   _____

3. Think about the games and toys being played today. Which games and toys do you think kids will still be playing a hundred years from now? Why?

   _____

   _____

4. What new game or toy do you think will be invented one hundred years from now?

   _____

   _____

New Champs Take the Court

Two sisters are U.S. tennis champs. Serena Williams beat last year's U.S. Open champ in a very hard match. Serena's sister is Venus Williams. Venus is also a tough tennis player.

Serena and Venus sometimes play as teammates. It is called "doubles." They win many times. Serena is also a "singles" champ. The two sisters are "doubles" champs!

They are very good athletes. But Serena says, "Tennis is a game. It is not your life. We believe in family."

New Champs Take the Court *(cont.)*

Directions: Answer these questions. You may look at the story.

1. What are the sisters' names?

    a. Senus and Verena

    b. Venus and Serena

    c. Jupiter and Mars

2. What sport do the sisters play?

    a. They play hockey.

    b. They play golf.

    c. They play tennis.

3. What is so special about the sisters?

    _____

    _____

4. Compare tennis to another sport that uses a ball. How are the sports alike? How are the sports different?

    _____

    _____

5. What does it take to become a top tennis player?

    _____

    _____

6. Would you rather play against one player or would you rather play doubles against another team? Why?

    _____

    _____

7. Tell why the U.S. Open is so difficult to win.

    _____

    _____

8. Serena won almost one million dollars at the U.S. Open. Should athletes be paid that much money for winning a game? Explain why or why not.

    _____

    _____

New Champs Take the Court *(cont.)*

Directions: Look at the graph. Answer the questions.

U.S. Open Single's Prize Money (Women)

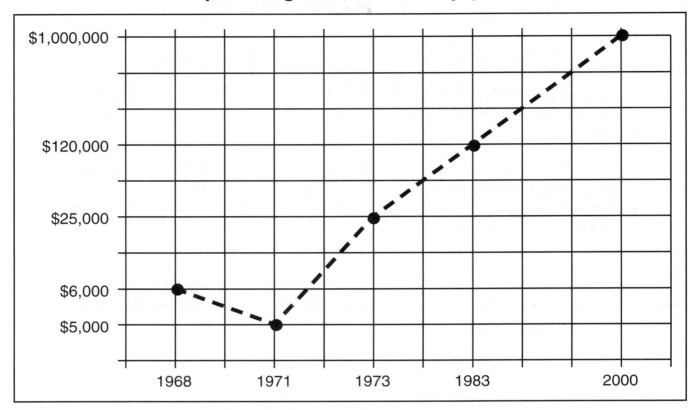

1. What was the top prize money in 1968?

   _____

   _____

2. What happened to the prize money from 1983 to 2000? Why do you think this has happened?

   _____

   _____

3. What do you think will happen to the prize money over the next few years?

   _____

   _____

4. What impact will the change in prize money have on tennis fans?

   _____

   _____

Kid Power

Kids find ways to make where we live a better place.

A hurricane hit the island of Puerto Rico. The storm wiped out many trees. Some third graders wanted to help. They planted new trees.

Kids in New Jersey learned that birds were losing their homes. They wanted to help the birds. The New Jersey class made calendars. Then they sold them. The boys and girls used the money to make homes for birds.

Kid Power *(cont.)*

Directions: Answer these questions. You may look at the story.

1. What did the kids do to raise money?
   a. They made and sold calendars.
   b. They sold trees.
   c. They sold birds.

2. What happened in Puerto Rico?
   a. There was a volcano.
   b. There was a tornado.
   c. There was a hurricane.

3. What kinds of things do birds need?

   _____

   _____

4. What can kids do to make the world a better place?

   _____

   _____

5. Define "kid power."

   _____

   _____

6. How do you think the kids felt after they worked on one of the projects?

   _____

   _____

7. Why are kids interested in making the world a better place?

   _____

   _____

8. Should kids be required to do community service as part of their citizenship grade? Why or why not?

   _____

   _____

Kid Power _(cont.)_

Directions: Look at the picture. Answer the questions.

1. Where are these kids?

   _____

   _____

2. List the things the kids are doing to help.

   _____

   _____

3. How will the kids' work help the community?

   _____

   _____

4. What would happen if kids in other communities worked to keep parks beautiful and clean?

   _____

   _____

Hotshot on a Skateboard

Ryan Sheckler knows what he wants to be when he grows up. He knew at his sixth birthday party. Ryan asked Tony Hawk to his party. Hawk is a skateboard champ. Hawk came after Ryan said he could have a piece of cake.

After meeting Hawk, Ryan knew he wanted to be a skateboarder. "I want to be on posters," says Ryan.

Ryan may get his wish. He won a contest in California. Ryan did a move called the Wave Gap. Ryan zoomed off a 14-foot-high ramp. He went through the air. Then he landed on a wooden hill six feet away.

Watch out for Ryan Sheckler. You might see him on a poster!

Hotshot on a Skateboard *(cont.)*

Directions: Answer these questions. You may look at the story.

1. When did Ryan decide that he wanted to be a skateboarder?

    a. He decided at his sixth birthday party.

    b. He decided when he was born.

    c. He decided when he was grown up.

2. Who is Tony Hawk?

    a. He is a party planner.

    b. He is a skateboard champ.

    c. He is Ryan's cousin.

3. Tell the steps for doing the "Wave Gap."

    _____

    _____

4. Why does Ryan want to be a skateboarder?

    _____

    _____

5. What safety measures can a skateboarder take to prevent injuries?

    _____

    _____

6. What does a person need to know and need to have in order to be great at skateboarding?

    _____

    _____

7. What is so special about being on a poster?

    _____

    _____

8. Is skateboarding a real sport?

    _____

    _____

Hotshot on a Skateboard *(cont.)*

Directions: Look at the graph. Answer the questions.

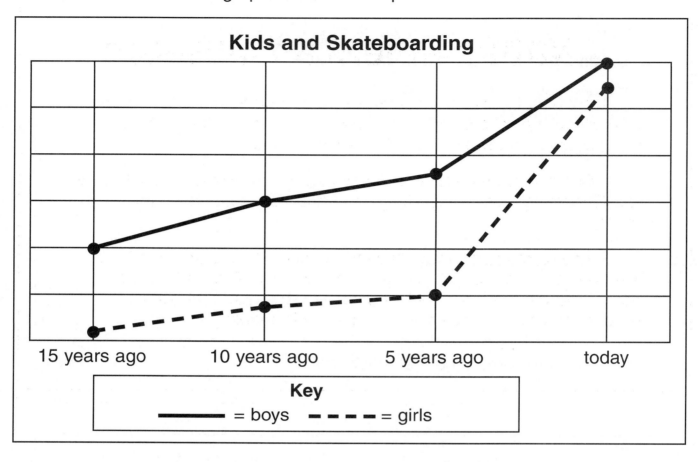

Kids and Skateboarding

15 years ago   10 years ago   5 years ago   today

Key

——— = boys   - - - - - = girls

1. What has happened to the number of kids who like to skateboard?

_____

_____

2. How do the number of girls compare to the number of boys who like to skateboard?

_____

_____

3. What factors have contributed to the increased number of kids who skateboard?

_____

_____

4. What new innovations will be made to the skateboards of the future?

_____

_____

A Native American Museum

In 1999, Native Americans met in Washington, D.C. They met where a museum is being built. The museum will tell about the many tribes. The Native Americans were happy.

Ben Nighthorse Campbell was happy, too. He is a senator. He is a Cheyenne. He worked to get the museum built. It was his dream.

The chief of one tribe blessed the site. At one time his tribe lived on the same site. "The water is still here. The earth is still here. And we are still here," he said. He was glad that Native Americans have a place to remember their people.

A Native American Museum (cont.)

Directions: Answer these questions. You may look at the story.

1. Where did the Native Americans in the story go?
   a. Cheyenne
   b. Washington state
   c. Washington, D.C.

2. Who is Ben Nighthorse Campbell?
   a. He is a senator.
   b. He is a chief.
   c. He is a museum worker.

3. What was Campbell's dream?

   _____

   _____

4. Why was the museum so important to the Native Americans?

   _____

   _____

5. What was special about the site?

   _____

   _____

6. What other things can museums recognize and share?

   _____

   _____

7. What does the blessing mean?

   _____

   _____

8. Why should museums recognize and share different cultures?

   _____

   _____

A Native American Museum *(cont.)*

Directions: Read the blessing. Answer the questions.

Blessing

The water is still here.

The earth is still here.

And we are still here.

---

1. What things does the blessing say are still here?

_____

_____

2. Who is "we" in the blessing?

_____

_____

3. Why was the Native American museum site blessed with this blessing?

_____

_____

4. What other phrases could be added to the blessing?

_____

_____

Happy Holidays!

Which holiday do you like the best?

Some people like the Fourth of July. A lot of kids march in parades on that day.

People from India say hello to the new year. They light candles. They wear flowers, too.

The Chinese welcome the new year, too. They have a parade. Some people dress up as dragons.

Kids in New Mexico dress up for a special holiday. The kids dress like people who lived a long time ago. The kids are proud of who they are.

In Mexico, May Fifth is a holiday. Lots of people dance on that day. They eat good food, too.

We all like holidays. Holidays bring us together.

Happy Holidays! *(cont.)*

Directions: Answer these questions. You may look at the story.

1. Name a holiday mentioned in the story.
   a. Christmas
   b. Halloween
   c. Fourth of July

2. Which holidays does the story say have parades?
   a. May Fifth and Fourth of July
   b. Indian New Year and Chinese New Year
   c. Fourth of July and Chinese New Year

3. How is the Chinese New Year celebrated?

   _____

   _____

4. Which holiday do you like the best? Why?

   _____

   _____

5. What makes a holiday a holiday?

   _____

   _____

6. Explain why different cultures celebrate the same holiday in different ways.

   _____

   _____

7. What would it be like if everybody celebrated the same holidays in the same ways?

   _____

   _____

8. Should holidays be recognized and celebrated in school?

   _____

   _____

Happy Holidays! *(cont.)*

Directions: Look at the pictures. Answer the questions.

1. What holidays do these things represent?

   _____

   _____

2. Name three holidays that you know or celebrate.

   _____

   _____

3. How come some holidays also mean a "no school day" and others do not? How do you think it is decided?

   _____

   _____

4. Every once in a while, a new holiday is added to the calendar.   For example, a special holiday was added to recognize the important contributions of Martin Luther King, Jr., and now there is a Martin Luther King, Jr. Day. What holiday would you like to see added to the calendar? Why?

   _____

   _____

Play Time

It is hard work to put on a play. But the people who do it make it look easy.

Directors tell the actors where to move. They tell them how to say their lines. "Talk more slowly," the director might say.

Costumers think up the costumes. Then they fit them on the actors. Many people help make them.

Is the play set inside a house? Is it set by the sea? The set builders can build it!

The light people light the stage during the play. They can turn day into night or night into day. The sound people run the sound. They help us hear the actors.

Who else is needed for the play? You are! Actors need you to come see it.

Play Time *(cont.)*

Directions: Answer these questions. You may look at the story.

1. What are "lines"?
   a. They are what the costumers say.
   b. They are what the actors say.
   c. They are what the directors say.

2. What does the costumer need to know?
   a. The costumer needs to know how to sew.
   b. The costumer needs to know how to act.
   c. The costumer needs to know how to build a set.

3. What does a director do?

   _____

   _____

4. Name the people who put on a play.

   _____

   _____

5. How is a movie like a play?

   _____

   _____

6. What do successful plays have in common?

   _____

   _____

7. What happens if the play got bad reviews?

   _____

   _____

8. Who is more important in a play, the actors or the director?

   _____

   _____

Play Time *(cont.)*

Directions: Look at the picture. Answer the questions.

1. What is the play's title?

   _____

   _____

2. Where does it take place?

   _____

   _____

3. Make a list of characters or other items that might be used in the play.

   _____

   _____

4. If this play is a hit with audiences and critics, what do you think will happen next?

   _____

   _____

For One or More Players

My best friend Kristen moved to Oregon. You know what that means? She can't play with me on the playground anymore. The other kids all have best friends who still live here. They can play with each other. So, now during recess I make up games to play by myself. They are all for one person.

One of these games is "Bouncing Beth Bumbledown." That's a game where you try to jump higher than a bouncing ball.

Some kids think I'm a nut. My dad says, "Without nuts we wouldn't have Rocky Road ice cream."

Today, two girls asked me what game I was playing. Maybe tomorrow I'll explain it to them. Then I can make up games for two or more.

For One or More Players *(cont.)*

Directions: Answer these questions. You may look at the story.

1. What was the name of the game she invented?
    a. For One or More Players
    b. Nuts
    c. Bouncing Beth Bumbledown

2. Why did she make up games for one player?
    a. Her best friend moved away.
    b. She didn't like the other kids.
    c. She thinks playing alone is best.

3. What other games can be played with one person?

    _____

    _____

4. Why does her dad think that being a "nut" is important?

    _____

    _____

5. Why would she need to make up games for two or more players?

    _____

    _____

6. Why did the girls ask her to play with them?

    _____

    _____

7. What if your best friend moved away? What would you do?

    _____

    _____

8. Describe the qualities found in a good friend.

    _____

    _____

For One or More Players *(cont.)*

Directions: Read the game directions. Answer the questions.

How to Play "Bouncing Beth Bumbledown"

1. Stand on the blacktop or cement.

2. Take a big, rubber, bouncing ball and bounce it as hard as you can.

3. When the ball bounces back up, jump up in the air. Try to jump higher than the ball.

---

1. What is the name of the game?

   _____

   _____

2. How many players play the game?

   _____

   _____

3. What makes the game for one kid only?

   _____

   _____

4. How can the game be changed so that two or three kids can play it together?

   _____

   _____

Bringing Up Baby

Many animals take care of their babies.

Kittens are born with their eyes closed. The mother cat looks after her babies.

A mother hen has chicks. The chicks do what the mother hen does. That is how they learn to peck for food.

A mother lion picks up her cub by the fur on its neck. She takes it to a safe place.

Baby elephants weigh 150 pounds when they are born. Their mothers lead them around with their trunks.

Playing helps baby animals grow strong. Puppies spend much of their time playing. Sometimes they trip over their own feet!

Bringing Up Baby *(cont.)*

Directions: Answer these questions. You may look at the story.

1. What are a cat's babies called?

   a. puppies

   b. chicks

   c. kittens

2. What are some of the things parents do to take care of their babies?

   _____

   _____

3. How do babies learn to do things?

   _____

   _____

4. Compare human babies to animal babies.

   _____

   _____

5. How do animal parents communicate with their babies?

   _____

   _____

6. What would happen to animal babies if their parents were not able to take care of them?

   _____

   _____

7. Why is playing an important part of learning for animal babies?

   _____

   _____

8. Why is it important for animal babies to learn from their parents instead of from people?

   _____

   _____

Bringing Up Baby (cont.)

Directions: Look at the pictures. Answer the questions.

1. Name the animals in the pictures.

   _____

   _____

2. Which animals from the pictures do you think need the most care? Why?

   _____

   _____

3. Make a list of the different ways that parent animals can communicate with their babies.

   _____

   _____

4. How are the ways the animals travel like the ways that humans and their babies travel? How could these ways be improved?

   _____

   _____

A Letter to the White House

Dear Mr. President,

I am in the first grade at Green Hills School. We are learning about tide pools. Last week we went to the ocean. We saw tide pools, but there were no animals in them. The pools were full of dirty water.

Our teacher told us about laws against putting bad things in the water. Will you please help make stronger laws? Then we can have clean water. The animals will come back to the tide pools.

Yours truly,

Kayla Low

A Letter to the White House (cont.)

Directions: Answer these questions. You may look at the story.

1. Who did Kayla write a letter to?
    a. the president
    b. the tide pool people
    c. her teacher

2. What is the president's job?
    a. The president runs the schools.
    b. The president runs the country.
    c. The president runs the tide pools.

3. What is Kayla concerned about? Why?

_____

_____

4. What kinds of laws could be passed to protect the tide pools?

_____

_____

5. On the back of this paper, draw a picture of the tide pools before and after laws were passed.

6. What factors have harmed the tide pools?

_____

_____

7. What would happen if the tide pools became dirtier?

_____

_____

8. Should there be laws to protect the tide pools?

_____

_____

A Letter to the White House (cont.)

Directions: Read the signs. Answer the questions.

1. What are these?

_____

_____

2. What do they have in common?

_____

_____

3. Why should people obey the messages here? What would happen if they did not?

_____

_____

4. Write a new sign to keep nature clean and safe.

_____

_____

My Trip on a Plane

I went on a plane trip by myself. Mom said, "You are old enough to visit Aunt Jan on your own." Mom took me to the airport. I was a little scared. I did not mind when she gave me a goodbye kiss.

Stan, the flight attendant, showed me my seat on the plane. I was so excited I could not sit still. The man in front of me said, "Please stop kicking my seat."

The plane's engines roared. Before I knew it, we were flying.

Stan gave me a book of puzzles. The fluffy clouds below us looked like marshmallows.

The plane landed in Cleveland. Stan took me off the plane. Aunt Jan was waiting for me. I was excited to see her. I did not mind when she gave me a hello kiss.

My Trip on a Plane *(cont.)*

Directions: Answer these questions. You may look at the story.

1. Who was she going to see?
   a. Aunt Jan
   b. Mom
   c. Stan

2. What was the flight attendant's name?
   a. Aunt Jan
   b. Mom
   c. Stan

3. Why was she flying by herself? How did she feel at first?

   _____

   _____

4. What does a flight attendant do?

   _____

   _____

5. What could the airlines do to make air travel more "kid friendly"?

   _____

   _____

6. Why didn't she care when her mother kissed her goodbye or when her aunt kissed her hello?

   _____

   _____

7. What if her aunt was late picking her up? What could she do?

   _____

   _____

8. Do you think kids should fly on planes by themselves?

   _____

   _____

My Trip on a Plane *(cont.)*

Directions: Look at the picture. Answer the questions.

1. Name the method of transportation.

   _____

   _____

2. What is the name of the airline?

   _____

   _____

3. Why would a person choose to fly instead of taking a train, riding on a bus, or driving in a car?

   _____

   _____

4. First people traveled by foot and by horse. Then came ships, trains, cars, and planes. How do you think people will travel in the future?

   _____

   _____

The Bears Bounce Back

At one time there were 100,000 grizzly bears in the U.S. Now there are about 1,000. (This does not count the bears in Alaska.) A law was made in 1975. The law did not let people hurt the bears or the bears' homes.

The plan is working. Today, there are a lot of bears. Most of the bears live in the Yellowstone National Park.

There are times when the bears leave Yellowstone National Park. The bears might kill sheep or cows. Some people are scared. They want to shoot a bear that may hurt them. But some people think there are too few bears. They want to keep helping the bears. People and bears need to get along.

The Bears Bounce Back *(cont.)*

Directions: Answer these questions. You may look at the story.

1. Where do most of the grizzly bears live?

   a. the zoo

   b. Yellowstone National Park

   c. Alaska

2. Why are people afraid of bears?

   a. They think bears will hurt them.

   b. They think bears will hurt their cars.

   c. They think bears will hurt their homes.

3. What changes have allowed the number of grizzly bears to increase?

   _____

   _____

4. What can people and bears do so that they can get along with each other?

   _____

   _____

5. What caused the number of bears to get smaller?

   _____

   _____

6. Should people be afraid of bears? Should bears be afraid of people?

   _____

   _____

7. What might have happened to the grizzly bears if the law had not been passed in 1975?

   _____

   _____

8. Do you think it is important that the grizzly bears continue to be protected by laws?

   _____

   _____

The Bears Bounce Back *(cont.)*

Directions: Look at the graph. Answer the questions.

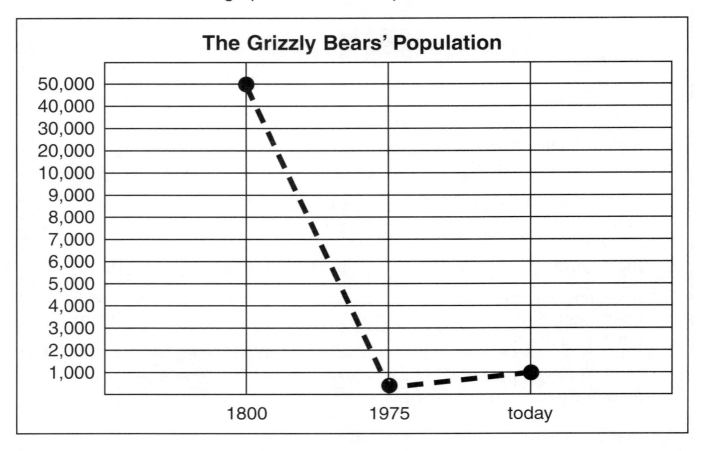

1. Approximately how many bears were there in the 1800s?

   _____

   _____

2. What happened to the bear population before and after 1975?

   _____

   _____

3. If the grizzly bears continue to be protected, what do you think will happen to their numbers? What might happen if the grizzly bears stop being protected?

   _____

   _____

4. As people build more and more homes, businesses, and roads in areas that were once only inhabited by bears and other wildlife, what will this do to the bears?

   _____

   _____

She Takes the Cake!

Mmmmm . . . Claudia Fleming has a sweet life. At the end of the day, she is covered with sugar and dotted with chocolate. She is a pastry chef. She works at a restaurant in New York City. She makes desserts all day.

"It is like putting on a play," she says. "You get ready all morning. The curtain goes up for lunch and dinner. It is time for the show!"

Claudia started by being a helper. She watched her boss. Soon she was the boss herself. She says that kids who want to be chefs should read cookbooks. "Cook at home," she says. "Work any job in a restaurant."

The best part of her job? "Making something," she says, "and then making someone happy with it."

She Takes the Cake! *(cont.)*

Directions: Answer these questions. You may look at the story.

1. What kinds of books should kids read if they want to cook when they grow up?

   a. storybooks

   b. grown-up books

   c. cookbooks

2. What are pastries?

   a. desserts

   b. lunch foods

   c. dinner foods

3. Invent a new dessert. What does it look like? What does it taste like? How is it made? What will it be called?

   _____

   _____

4. Where else can recipes be found besides in a cookbook?

   _____

   _____

5. Explain why Claudia Fleming's life is so "sweet."

   _____

   _____

6. What kinds of things would you need to know in order to become a good pastry chef? How are these same skills used in another job?

   _____

   _____

7. Write a "recipe" for becoming a pastry chef.

   _____

   _____

8. Judge what makes an ordinary dessert a yummy dessert.

   _____

   _____

She Takes the Cake! *(cont.)*

Directions: Read the recipe. Answer the questions.

Chocolate Milk

Ingredients:
- 8 ounces of cold milk
- 1 heaping teaspoon of cocoa powder

Materials:
- 1 glass
- 1 long spoon
- 1 napkin

Directions:

Fill a tall glass with milk. Add the dried cocoa powder to the glass of milk. Using a long spoon, stir the dried cocoa powder in the milk until all of the powder is gone. Drink and enjoy!

1. What is the item above called?

_____

2. What would happen if one of the ingredients were left out?

_____

_____

3. What skills are used when following the recipe?

_____

_____

4. In what other jobs or tasks are these same skills used?

_____

_____

Don't Ever Kiss a Peacock!

I went to my friend Jaime's birthday party. It was at the zoo. We saw a baby giraffe. It could run and it was only five days old.

A monkey was in the next habitat. His name was Bonzo. I wanted to feed Bonzo cotton candy. My friend Jaime said, "No, that will make him sick."

Then we walked to a big cage. Five beautiful peacocks were inside. They were many colors. They had long feathers. I wanted to see them better. I put my face very close to the cage. A peacock bit my nose! I jumped back. My nose hurt. After a second, I was okay.

Jaime's mom smiled. She said, "Don't ever kiss a peacock!"

Don't Ever Kiss a Peacock! *(cont.)*

Directions: Answer these questions. You may look at the story.

1. What was the friend's name?

 a. Joey

 b. Jaime

 c. Jane

2. Where was the birthday party held?

 a. at Jaime's house

 b. at the park

 c. at the zoo

3. Why shouldn't people feed the animals?

 _____

 _____

4. Describe a peacock.

 _____

 _____

5. On the back of this paper, design the perfect habitat for a peacock. Tell about the habitat and why a peacock would like to live there.

 _____

 _____

6. What makes a peacock beautiful?

 _____

 _____

7. Why do you think the peacock "kissed" the person telling the story?

 _____

 _____

8. Do you think animals enjoy being in a zoo?

 _____

 _____

Don't Ever Kiss a Peacock! *(cont.)*

Directions: Look at the picture. Read the signs. Answer the questions.

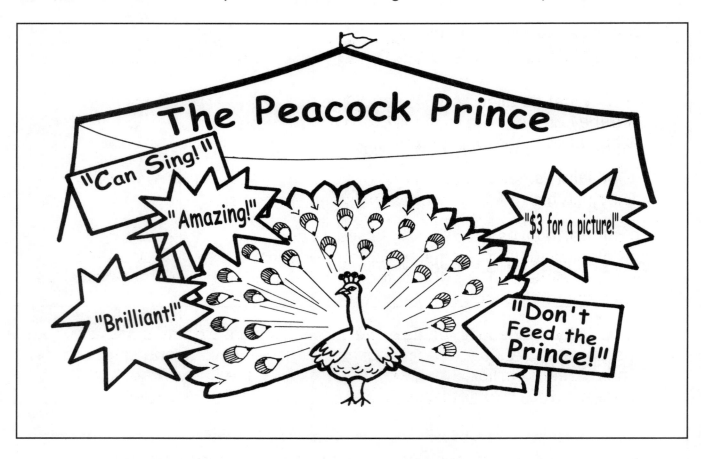

1. Name the animal.

   _____

2. Where do you think the animal lives? What makes you say that?

   _____

   _____

3. What is the point in having all of the signs around the animal?

   _____

   _____

4. What would happen if all of the animals in the zoo had their own signs? Is it a good idea?

   _____

   _____

Hello! Anybody Out There?

What do aliens from outer space look like? Are they short? Are they green? Are they tall? Are they purple? Are there really aliens at all? Today science has the tools to look for life in space.

How do scientists look for aliens? They listen very carefully. They use big radio telescopes to listen for signals from space.

Earth gives off billions of signals each day. Maybe creatures on other planets give off signals, too. The telescopes pick up all kinds of signals. Then computers sort through them. They look for ones that did not come from Earth.

Why do we look for life? We want to know if we are alone in the universe. After all, Earth is only one planet, circling one star. There are 400 billion other stars in our galaxy, the Milky Way. And there are 100 billion other galaxies! Do you think we're alone?

Hello! Anybody Out There? *(cont.)*

Directions: Answer these questions. You may look at the story.

1. What tools do scientists use to search for aliens?

    a. big radio telescopes and computers

    b. television cameras

    c. spaceships

2. What is our galaxy called?

    a. the Milky Way

    b. the Hershey Bar

    c. the Big Dipper

3. Compare yourself to an alien. How are you alike? How are you different?

    _____

    _____

4. What do you think an alien might look like? Write a sentence telling about the alien.

    _____

    _____

5. What could aliens learn from people? What could people learn from aliens?

    _____

    _____

6. What if there really were aliens? What kinds of things would be important for earth people to share with the aliens?

    _____

    _____

7. Are there really aliens? Explain your answer.

    _____

    _____

8. Is it important to search for other forms of life? Why or why not?

    _____

    _____

Hello! Anybody Out There? *(cont.)*

Directions: Look at the graph. Answer the questions.

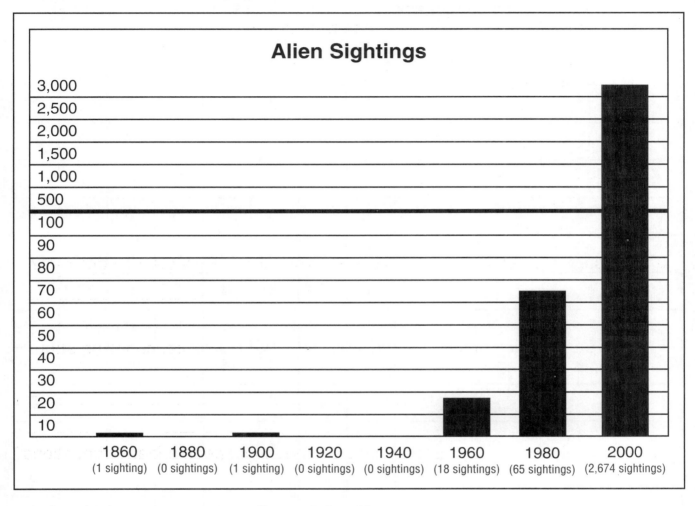

Alien Sightings

Year	Sightings
1860	(1 sighting)
1880	(0 sightings)
1900	(1 sighting)
1920	(0 sightings)
1940	(0 sightings)
1960	(18 sightings)
1980	(65 sightings)
2000	(2,674 sightings)

1. In which years were no aliens sighted?

   _____

2. What do you think caused the number of alien sightings to increase from 1960 to 2000?

   _____

   _____

3. Aliens are usually described as little green men with long skinny arms and fingers. Why do you think aliens are described in this way?

   _____

   _____

4. Based on the information shown on the graph, what do you think will happen to the number of aliens sighted in 2020?

   _____

   _____

Student Achievement Graph

Use this page to keep track of the number of questions answered correctly. Color in a box for each correct answer. (Duplicate this page as necessary.)

Lesson	1	2	3	4	5	6	7	8
	1	2	3	4	5	6	7	8
	1	2	3	4	5	6	7	8
	1	2	3	4	5	6	7	8
	1	2	3	4	5	6	7	8
	1	2	3	4	5	6	7	8
	1	2	3	4	5	6	7	8
	1	2	3	4	5	6	7	8
	1	2	3	4	5	6	7	8
	1	2	3	4	5	6	7	8
	1	2	3	4	5	6	7	8
	1	2	3	4	5	6	7	8
	1	2	3	4	5	6	7	8
	1	2	3	4	5	6	7	8
	1	2	3	4	5	6	7	8
	1	2	3	4	5	6	7	8
	1	2	3	4	5	6	7	8
	1	2	3	4	5	6	7	8
	1	2	3	4	5	6	7	8
	1	2	3	4	5	6	7	8
	1	2	3	4	5	6	7	8

Answer Key

Many of the answers will show an example of how the students might respond. For many of the questions there may be more than one correct answer.

page 13
1. a
2. b
3. b
4. The students' attendance and grades will continue to improve, and they will have less trouble with the law.
5. (Student draws a picture.)
6. The students' behavior will improve. Student school attendance and grades will improve.
7. Answers will vary.
8. The kids knew that there was somebody who would be watching them and holding them accountable for their behavior.
9. Evidence includes the students' report cards, disciplinary notes and phone calls home, less truancy, better attendance, better grades, etc.

page 14
1. That fewer students were in trouble. It changed because Officer Sinclair was watching them.
2. The students know that Officer Sinclair will be checking with their principal and with their teachers.
3. The students' grades improved because they were at school every day, ready to learn.
4. Answers will vary.

page 16
1. c
2. a
3. b
4. Answers will vary.
5. She means that sometimes at work you are constantly being interrupted by other people or by phone calls.
6. Answers will vary.
7. Sometimes there are a lot of interruptions at school or a classmate wants to talk instead of work.
8. The mother had to know the stuff to do her job. The child didn't know what the grown-ups were talking about or why it was important.

page 17
1. The skills include knowing how to use a calculator, having good math skills, knowing how to use a computer, and having good people skills.
2. "People skills" are knowing how to get along with other people, being friendly and helpful to others.
3. An accountant needs to know how to add and subtract.
4. The accountant will need to take classes and do a lot of reading to keep up to date.

page 19
1. b
2. a
3. a
4. Answers will vary.

page 19 (second column)
5. If a team had more dogs it might finish the race sooner. If a team had fewer dogs it might take the team longer to finish the race.
6. Horses wouldn't be able to pull the sleds for many days through all of the snow and ice.
7. Answers will vary.
8. Answers will vary.

page 20
1. It begins in Anchorage and ends in Nome.
2. They are about 20-30 miles apart. The race is divided so that teams can rest.
3. There are cabins to mark the way.
4. Answers will vary.

page 22
1. a
2. b
3. c
4. Lake Champlain was made by glaciers. It is linked to the Great Lakes by rivers.
5. The lakes had to be made from glaciers and they have to be big.
6. Answers will vary.
7. He wanted some of the money the government gives to states to study the Great Lakes.
8. Answers will vary.

page 23
1. They are Lake Superior, Lake Michigan, Lake Huron, Lake Erie, and Lake Ontario.
2. The states are Minnesota, Wisconsin, Michigan, Illinois, Indiana, Ohio, Pennsylvania, New York.
3. Lake Ontario is the smallest. Lake Superior is the largest. From smallest to largest they are Lake Ontario, Lake Erie, Lake Huron, Lake Michigan, and Lake Superior.
4. Answers will vary.

page 25
1. c
2. a
3. The flutes were made from hollowed out bird bones.
4. Other instruments include drums, guitars, cymbals, flutes, recorders, tambourines, etc.
5. Answers will vary.
6. Answers will vary.
7. Answers will vary.
8. Evidence includes how far the instruments are buried under ground, the materials that they are made from, the location where they are found, drawings on walls and in books, etc.

page 26
1. There are seven holes.
2. There were probably a lot of birds that were easy to catch.
3. Probably something sharp that could have been used to carve the bones.
4. Answers will vary.

page 28
1. c
2. a
3. Pictures and answers will vary.
4. Answers will vary.

5. The book was probably written so that people can know it is okay to feel happy or sad.
6. Answers will vary.
7. Answers will vary.
8. Answers will vary.

page 29
1. an apple
2. seeds for eyes, stem for nose, and indentation for mouth
3. Anger is shown by the mouth and slant of the eyes.
4. Answers will vary.
5. Answers will vary.

page 31
1. c
2. b
3. a
4. Pictures will vary.
5. Answers will vary.
6. They put her back because they know that whales need to swim all over the ocean.
7. Answers will vary.
8. Answers will vary.

page 32
1. about 45-50 feet
2. A whale has flippers and fins and a body like a fish, so it looks like it belongs in the water.
3. Answers will vary.
4. Answers will vary.

page 34
1. c
2. c
3. b
4. Pictures will vary.
5. Hunters killed the tigers. The rest of the answer will vary, although the best answer suggests that the hunters used the tigers for many things (such as clothes, medicine, and souvenirs).
6. People have set aside lands for the tigers. They have food and are safe from hunters.
7. Answers will vary.
8. Answers will vary.

page 35
1. largest population = Bengal tiger; smallest living population = South China tiger
2. They are extinct. Hunters killed them all.
3. Answers will vary.
4. Answers will vary. Sample animals include dinosaurs, dodo birds, and tigers.

page 37
1. b
2. c
3. a
4. Answers will vary.
5. Answers will vary, although a likely answer is that other items might be food, clothing, and favorite pets. These were items that were important to the people.
6. They were probably buried so that people would have things to use in the afterlife.
7. They had been left alone since they were first buried. They were preserved well in the mummifying process.

Answer Key (cont.)

page 37 (*cont.*)
8. Answers will vary.

page 38
1. Likely tools and supplies may have included stones, sand, rocks, knives, and axes.
2. Accept any reasonable answer, although people probably used ropes to pull them to where they were needed.
3. Answers will vary.

page 40
1. a
2. c
3. Answers may include the following: Mastodons and elephants are both big mammals with tusks. They can move heavy objects. They wouldn't have had very many enemies. The mastodon is extinct. The elephant is still living.
4. Answers will vary.
5. Other things include plants, people, other kinds of animals, and anything that was once living.
6. They can match it to known fossils.
7. They can determine such things as how long ago it became fossilized, how it lived, what it might have looked like, etc.
8. Answers will vary.

page 41
1. the head
2. It belonged to a dinosaur.
3. You can tell something about what the animal looked like, what it ate, when it might have lived, how it might have died, and how big it might have been.
4. Answers and pictures will vary.

page 43
1. a
2. b
3. Answers may include the following: Buses and trucks are both big, they can carry many people, they have doors, they have windows, and they have the same parts. Buses can carry a lot more people than trucks. Buses do not have seatbelts. Trucks have seatbelts. Buses carry items under the seats. Trucks carry items in the bed of the truck or pull them behind the truck.
4. Larry knew where the brakes were on the truck, so he knew where the brakes were on the bus. Larry knew that the brakes are used to stop a vehicle.
5. Answers will vary.
6. It is not often that someone his age would know what to do in an emergency.
7. Answers may include the following: The bus could have been in a serious accident. People could have been hurt. The bus could have hit a car or people.
8. Answers will vary.

page 44
1. It is a bus. It is used to take people from one place to another.
2. Students can get out through the windows, the doors, the side doors, or the back.

3. Answers will vary, although a likely answer may include that it might be safer to stay on the bus if it is dark or the weather is bad or if the students might hurt themselves trying to get off of the bus.
4. Answers will vary.

page 46
1. c
2. b
3. c
4. An ankylosaur had plates on its back and was 30 feet long. It used its tail like a club. It ate plants.
5. Its enemies were probably bigger dinosaurs and meat-eating dinosaurs.
6. They are probably special because the bones were 95 million years old and were in North America earlier than scientists had thought.
7. Answers will vary.
8. Answers will vary.

page 47
1. Enemies were probably larger dinosaurs and meat-eating dinosaurs.·
2. It could fly away or bite or peck with its beak.
3. A bird is similar. They both can fly and they both have sharp beaks. The pterodactyl was much larger than the birds we know today. The pterodactyl is extinct.

page 49
1. b
2. c
3. Answers may include the following: They both have beds and different rooms. The ice hotel melts every year and does not have heat. A regular hotel room has regular beds, furniture, heat, and televisions.
4. Answers and pictures will vary.
5. Tools probably include chisels, hammers, and wheelbarrows to haul away the extra snow and ice.
6. Answers will vary.
7. The Arctic or Antarctic are the likely answers. The rest of the answer will vary.
8. Answers will vary.

page 50
1. It is an igloo.
2. Answers will vary but may include the following: The house is made of blocks of snow. The people cut the snow into blocks and stack them to make the igloo. A piece of frozen water is used to make a sky light.
3. Answers will vary but will probably include the ideas that the people are warm and cozy, they do not have to wear heavy clothing, and that there is a fire to cook over and to keep the people warm.
4. This type of house is made where there is a lot of snow. It is very cold there.
5. The house might last as long as the weather is cold enough to keep it from melting.

page 52
1. b
2. a
3. A water hyacinth is a green plant with purple flowers.

4. Answers will vary, but they will likely include that the Swamp Devil is "mean" and can chop up the plants. Suggested names will vary.
5. It spreads a carpet of flowers over the surface of the lake. The people are not able to fish and many of the natural lake plants and lake animals are not able to survive.
6. The aliens are the water hyacinths. They are aliens because they are "foreign"—they do not belong in Africa.
7. Answers will vary.
8. Answers will vary.

page 53
1. South America and Africa
2. The ways to travel are by boat or by plane. Traveling by plane would be the quickest way to travel. Traveling by boat would be the slowest way to travel.
3. Answers will vary.
4. Answers will vary.

page 55
1. b
2. c
3. Answers will vary.
4. Banks, stores, homes, and stadiums are some of the places that have guards or alarms. They help keep people and merchandise safe.
5. Guards and alarms are there to prevent people from stealing or damaging the different pieces of art.
6. Answers will vary.
7. The artwork can be damaged, broken, soiled by hands, scratched by people, etc.
8. Answers will vary.

page 56
1. C. Brown
2. the ocean, beach, or seashore
3. Materials listed may include tissue paper, sand, crayons, glitter, markers, sea shells, Scotch tape, glue, and paint.
4. Answers will vary.

page 58
1. a
2. c
3. Her dream was to be able to play with her friends on the equipment.
4. It means not to be able to do something in the same way as most other people.
5. Answers will vary but would include at least one of the following: learning, vision, hearing, and speech disabilities.
6. Answers will vary but will likely include the facts that both kinds of kids like to play, have fun, and have friends. All kids have feelings. All kids need love, food, shelter, clothing, and a family.
7. Answers will vary.
8. Answers will vary.

page 59
1. They are at a park.
2. The bars are too high, there are no seatbelts on the swings, there are stairs leading to the sandbox, there isn't a sidewalk for people in wheelchairs or who use crutches, and the bathrooms are not accessible to all people.

Answer Key (cont.)

page 59 (*cont.*)

3. Changes include that the swing seats can be lowered and have a seatbelt attached to them, the slide can have a ramp instead of a ladder, the sandbox can be moved so that it is level with the sidewalk, the bathrooms can be made bigger for all people to use, and the drinking fountains can be lowered.
4. Answers will vary.

page 61
1. b
2. a
3. In case something breaks, they need to know how to fix it.
4. Being underwater in a pool is like being "weightless" in space.
5. Answers may include science, math, engineering, mechanics, collecting and measuring data, operating the space craft, knowing how to keep in shape, knowing first aid, etc.
6. Answers will vary.
7. The other astronauts need to know how to take care of the person and what kind of medication or first aid to give.
8. Answers will vary.

page 62
1. Accept any three items from the packing list: 2 shirts with Velcro®, 2 pairs of shorts with Velcro®, 4 T-shirts with Velcro®, 2 pairs of pants with Velcro®, 1 pair of slipper socks, 1 flight jumpsuit, 1 sleeping bag with Velcro®, food in containers or bags with Velcro®, food tray with Velcro®.
2. It can be used to stick a person or an item to a stable object. It will keep the person or item from floating away.
3. Answers will vary.
4. Answers will vary.

page 64
1. c
2. a
3. If yes, each card has a special value or special skill that can be used to trap another Pokémon creature.
4. Answers will vary.
5. Pictures will vary.
6. Answers will vary but will likely include that kids like the characters and their names, and they like trading the cards.
7. Answers will vary.
8. Answers will vary.

page 65
1. 1934
2. Answers will vary.
3. Answers will vary.
4. Answers will vary.

page 67
1. b
2. c
3. They are tennis champs.
4. Answers will vary.
5. Answers will vary but will likely include that it takes a lot of effort, work, skill, training, support, coaching, practice, etc.

6. Answers will vary.
7. All of the top tennis players participate.
8. Answers will vary.

page 68
1. $6,000
2. It greatly increased. This is probably because tournaments want to attract top players.
3. Answers will vary.
4. Answers will vary.

page 70
1. a
2. c
3. Answers will vary but should include such things as food, water, and a clean and safe place to live (nest or cage).
4. Answers will vary.
5. Kid power is when kids unite to complete a job or accomplish a task. Together kids are strong.
6. They probably felt good and happy because someone or something benefited from their work.
7. Answers will vary.
8. Answers will vary.

page 71
1. They are at the park or a playground.
2. raking leaves, picking up trash, planting flowers, and helping younger kids play
3. Answers will vary but will likely include that the kids' work will keep the park clean and the landscape healthy and pretty. The community will be happy.
4. Answers will vary but will likely include that more and more people would take the time to visit the parks and would be more interested in keeping them clean and pretty themselves.

page 73
1. a
2. b
3. Roll down the ramp on the skateboard, shoot off the ramp and into the air, and land on the wooden hill 6 feet away.
4. He wants to be on a poster.
5. Answers may include the following: They can wear helmets, goggles, knee and elbow pads, and gloves. They can pay attention to their surroundings and what they are doing.
6. Answers will vary.
7. Usually only famous people are on posters.
8. Answers will vary.

page 74
1. More kids are skateboarding today than in the past.
2. At first not as many girls skateboarded as the boys. Now almost as many girls skateboard as boys.
3. Answers will vary but may include that the skateboards are "cool" looking, that skateboarding is a fun way to hang out with friends and practice new tricks, and that skateboarding is good exercise.
4. Answers will vary.

page 76
1. c
2. a
3. His dream was to build a museum to honor and recognize Native American culture and history.
4. The best answer is that it will give them an opportunity to remember their people.
5. At one time, Native Americans lived there.
6. Answers will vary.
7. Answers will vary.
8. Answers will vary.

page 77
1. It says that water, earth, and Native Americans (we) are still here.
2. "We" are the Native Americans.
3. Answers will vary.
4. Answers will vary.

page 79
1. c
2. c
3. It is celebrated with a parade and a dragon costume.
4. Answers will vary.
5. Answers will vary.
6. Answers will vary.
7. Answers will vary.
8. Answers will vary.

page 80
1. They represent Christmas, Halloween, and Thanksgiving.
2. Answers will vary.
3. Answers will vary.
4. Answers will vary.

page 82
1. b
2. a
3. He makes sure everyone knows their lines and where to stand.
4. Answers will include but are not limited to actors, directors, costumers, set builders, lighting people, and sound people.
5. Answers will vary.
6. Answers will vary.
7. Answers will vary.
8. Answers will vary.

page 83
1. *Fun in Cal-i-for-ny-a*
2. It takes place in the old west or wild west.
3. Answers may include cowboys, Indians, a sheriff, ladies, horses, cows, wagons, etc.
4. Answers will vary.

page 85
1. c
2. a
3. Answers may include hopscotch, jacks, shooting baskets, swinging, playing on the bars, etc.

Answer Key (cont.)

page 85 (cont.)

4. He thinks so because people are all different and that is what makes life more interesting and flavorful.
5. She wants to be friends with the girls who came over to talk to her.
6. Answers will vary but will likely include that the girls wanted to be her friend.
7. Answers will vary.
8. Answers will vary.

page 86

1. Bouncing Beth Bumbledown
2. one player
3. There is only one ball.
4. Answers will vary but may include that the game can be played to include more players by having all of the players jump up at the same time, by taking turns bouncing the ball and jumping, or by playing with more than one ball.

page 88

1. c
2. Answers may include that they take them to safe places, they show them how to hunt for food, and the mother looks after them.
3. Answers will vary but may include that they learn from their parents.
4. Answers will vary but may include that both human and animal babies need an adult to take care of them, to keep them safe, to keep them clean, and to show them how to take care of themselves. Animal mothers only care for their babies for a few years (at the most). Human babies need someone to care for them for many years.
5. Answers will vary but may include by growling, calling, swatting, and using body language.
6. Answers will vary but may include that the babies would probably not survive.
7. Answers will vary but may include playing is good exercise and they can practice their fighting skills.
8. Answers will vary.

page 89

1. kangaroos, birds, monkeys
2. Answers will vary.
3. Answers will vary but may include their voices, body language, trunks, paws, tails, etc.
4. Answers will vary.

page 91

1. a
2. b
3. She is concerned about the tide pools. The tide pools were dirty and there weren't any animals living in them.
4. Answers will vary but may include that laws can be passed to limit what kinds of things can be dumped into the oceans.
5. Pictures will vary.
6. Answers will vary.

7. Answers will vary.
8. Answers will vary.

page 92

1. They are signs.
2. They tell people what to do or what not to do.
3. The signs help keep people and animals safe. If the signs aren't followed, the people and animals could be sick or hurt.
4. Signs will vary.

page 94

1. a
2. c
3. Her mother felt she was old enough to travel by plane alone. She was nervous at first.
4. Answers may include one or more of the following: A flight attendant helps people get to their seats, stow luggage, serve food and beverages, meets the needs of the passengers, and helps people stay calm in case of an emergency.
5. Answers will vary.
6. Answers will vary.
7. Answers will vary.
8. Answers will vary.

page 95

1. an airplane or plane
2. Eagle Flights
3. Answers will vary but will likely include that it would be quicker to fly a long distance rather than traveling by bus, car, or train.
4. Answers will vary.

page 97

1. b
2. a
3. There was a law passed that protects grizzly bears and their homes.
4. Answers will vary.
5. People were hunting the grizzly bears.
6. Answers will vary.
7. The grizzly bears could have become extinct.
8. Answers will vary.

page 98

1. 50,000
2. Before 1975, the grizzly bear population was almost extinct. After 1975, the grizzly bear population is beginning to rise again.
3. Answers will vary.
4. Answers will vary.

page 100

1. c
2. a
3. Answers will vary.
4. Answers may include on boxes of food, in the newspaper, in magazines, and from television shows.
5. It is sweet because she works with a lot of sweet ingredients like sugar and chocolate. Also she is happy doing her work.
6. Answers may include reading, basic math

skills, different cooking skills, and using utensils. Reading and basic math skills are used in just about every kind of job on the market today.
7. Answers will vary.
8. Answers will vary.

page 101

1. a recipe
2. If one of the items were left out, the finished food item may not look right or taste good.
3. Reading and measuring (math) skills are used.
4. These same skills are used in just about every kind of job on the market today.

page 103

1. b
2. c
3. The food might make the animals sick.
4. A peacock is a bird with beautiful, colorful, long feathers.
5. Answers will vary.
6. Answers will vary.
7. The girl was invading the peacock's habitat.
8. Answers will vary.

page 104

1. It is a peacock.
2. It lives in a carnival or traveling circus show. We know because of the circus tent, all of the signs around it, and the fact that it costs $3 to have a picture of it.
3. The signs are there to attract people to come and see the peacock.
4. Answers will vary.

page 106

1. a
2. a
3. Answers will vary.
4. Answers will vary.
5. Answers will vary.
6. Answers will vary.
7. Answers will vary.
8. Answers will vary.

page 107

1. 1880, 1920, and 1940
2. Answers will vary but may include the following: People were becoming more interested in space. There were more planes, more weather balloons, and satellites in the air. The government was very secretive about these kinds of things, and there were movies being made about creatures from other planets.
3. Answers will vary but may include that they are probably described like this because one person described them that way and then everyone else copied him or her.
4. Answers will vary.